United Nations Office at Vienna
Centre for Social Development and Humanitarian Affairs

PARTICIPATION OF WOMEN IN DECISION-MAKING FOR PEACE: CASE-STUDY ON SWEDEN

Lindgren, Karin.

UNITED NATIONS

New York, 1989

NOTE

Symbols of United Nations documents are composed of capital letters combined with figures. Mention of such a symbol indicates a reference to a United Nations document.

The designations employed and the presentation of the material in this publication do not imply the expression of any opinion whatsoever on the part of the Secretariat of the United Nations concerning the legal status of any country, territory, city or area or of its authorities, or concerning the delimitation of its frontiers or boundaries.

ST/CSDHA/8

UNITED NATIONS PUBLICATION

Sales No.: E.89.IV.7

ISBN 92-1-130135-1

02700P

Foreword

This pilot case-study on Sweden is the first in a series of studies on the participation of women in decision-making processes related to peace and disarmament at the national, regional and world levels. The series will include case-studies analysing the issue in selected countries and in international forums, regional and global, for peace and disarmament matters.

The participation of women in decision-making processes has not yet been the subject of in-depth studies or analyses by the United Nations. However, government representatives expressed their interest in the subject on a number of occasions during the United Nations Decade for Women: Equality, Development and Peace, and the need for women to participate equally in decision-making was noted in such documents as the Convention on the Elimination of All Forms of Discrimination against Women (General Assembly resolution 34/180, annex), the Declaration on the Participation of Women in Promoting International Peace and Co-operation (General Assembly resolution 37/63, annex) and the Nairobi Forward-looking Strategies for the Advancement of Women. 1/ The Economic and Social Council, on the recommendation of the Commission on the Status of Women at its 1987 session, decided, in its resolution 1987/24, annex, to place the issue of the equal participation of women in political life, including decision-making and the promotion of peace, under two different priority themes, one being equality, in 1990, and the other being peace, in 1992.

It is a well-known if not always a well-documented fact that women have not been extensively involved in formulating and influencing the foreign policies of their countries, and their access to the diplomatic service and to institutions dealing with international relations remains subject to discriminatory practices. The precise situation is not known, however; nor has any specific attempt been made to identify the barriers preventing women from equal participation in the decision-making processes related to peace.

The primary objective of this pilot case-study is to present, in concrete, measurable terms, reliable data, specifically collected for the purpose, on the participation of women in decision-making processes related to peace and disarmament. The study has been carried out in a specific national context, in this case, Sweden. It provides analyses that will help to identify possible obstacles, and it makes recommendations for overcoming them. It can serve as a model for the elaboration of diagnostic studies in other countries.

The study can also serve as a guide to policy for Governments and international organizations in their efforts to implement the relevant provisions of the Declaration on the Participation of Women in Promoting International Peace and Co-operation and the Nairobi Forward-looking Strategies.

1/ Report of the World Conference to Review and Appraise the Achievements of the United Nations Decade for Women: Equality, Development and Peace, Nairobi, 15-26 July 1985 (United Nations publication, Sales No. E.85.IV.10), chap. I, sect. A.

The study was prepared in 1988 by Karin Lindgren, of the Department of Peace and Conflict Research, Uppsala University, Sweden, in her capacity as consultant to the Division for the Advancement of Women of the Centre for Social Development and Humanitarian Affairs, United Nations Office at Vienna. It was financed from a special trust fund for the monitoring and review and appraisal of the implementation of the Nairobi Forward-looking Strategies, on the basis of a grant from the Government of Sweden.

It is our hope that this type of objective, realistic and critical analysis will make a significant contribution towards achieving the goal set by the international community in the Nairobi Forward-looking Strategies: full equality between women and men by the year 2000.

Margaret J. Anstee
Director-General
United Nations Office at Vienna

CONTENTS

Tables

INTRODUCTION

A. Objectives

The primary objective of this study is to assess the participation of Swedish women in their country's decision-making processes related to peace and disarmament and to describe this participation in concrete, measurable terms. Another objective is to identify some of the obstacles that prevent women from achieving equal participation and to formulate recommendations for overcoming them. The study could give guidance to the Government and other policy-making bodies in Sweden. It could also serve as a source of information for women's groups and other organizations and could constitute a basis for further work by the United Nations in this area.

The fulfilment of the primary objective will shed light on who makes the decisions and on the point in the decision-making process at which they are made. In order to find out who makes the decisions, it is necessary to find out what the decisions are, which decision-making bodies are involved, and who within these bodies makes the decisions.

This study examines formal decisions taken at the national level relating, broadly, to peace and disarmament. The specific issues looked at are defence, disarmament, foreign affairs and foreign aid. The intention is to measure the influence of women on these issues at the highest decision-making levels.

The decision-making bodies studied are the Parliament (Riksdag), the Swedish Government and the central governmental authorities, as well as the diplomatic service and Swedish delegations abroad. It is the people holding formal decision-making positions within these bodies that are the subject of this study.

B. Decision-making processes

To learn at what point in the decision-making process crucial decisions relating to peace and disarmament are made, it is necessary to distinguish stages in the process. As mentioned above, the objective is to analyse the participation of women in these decisions. Although the emphasis is on the formal decision stage, other stages in the process are also discussed.

A decision-making process may be thought of as starting with an idea.* This idea may come from a non-governmental organization, from a grass-roots organization or from a research institute. It may also come from the media or from public or academic debate. Next, an organization works for the idea of acceptance and tries to bring pressure to bear on the political parties. The idea travels up the hierarchy of informal decision-making bodies until, finally, it reaches a formal decision-making body such as the Riksdag and becomes a formal decision.

_____

*The identification of the elements of decision-making processes is difficult, also there are different opinions among researchers on these processes. The model used here may not be complete, but it illustrates the elements of the process included in this study.

The evolution from idea to formal decision is important. It would be useful to know who formulated the idea in the first place, who brought pressure to bear on whom, and who decided what research was to be undertaken.

The formal decision has to be implemented, of course, by the central governmental bodies, and it is then expected to produce a result. It is interesting to examine this last stage of the decision-making process with regard to who is doing what, why, and for whom. If the desired result is not produced, the ideas for change may need to be reformulated, and the process may have to start again.

It would be of interest to ask when and where in this process women matter and how many decision makers, both formal and informal, are women. In decision-making processes related to peace and disarmament, it would be useful to know what role women play in the relevant non-governmental organizations, grass-roots organizations, peace movements and research institutes. Do they, for example, participate in formulating and implementing the programmes of the organizations? Do they formulate research programmes? How much influence do the activities of these organizations have on final decisions at the national level? While it is impossible to answer all these questions, it is important to point them out for future research, the need for which is great.

C. Methods of investigation

Female participation is examined in two ways, one quantitative, the other qualitative. First, the percentages and numbers of women and men in various decision-making bodies are presented (chapter I). The bodies are listed in the summary tables of the annex. To provide a picture of the change in female participation over time, data have been gathered for three years: 1966/67, 1976/77 and 1986/87.*

Secondly, a small number of decision makers have been interviewed (chapter II). The interviews were intended to elicit information on female participation, on possible obstacles to participation and on the advantages, in some cases, of being a woman. To identify all the obstacles, more research needs to be carried out.

Together, the two chapters will answer four questions:

(a) How did female participation change from 1966/67 to 1986/87? What, if any, trend is evident?

(b) Which positions within the decision-making bodies are normally held by women? Has the picture changed?

(c) Is female participation high or low in politically important decision-making bodies?

(d) Does the extent of female participation vary from issue to issue?

The important question, namely, whether participation implies influence and decision-making power, is discussed only briefly.

Each group of bodies covered in chapter I is treated in three subsections:

---

*A slash between dates indicates a legislative year.

(a) "Bodies examined", which describes the individual bodies;

(b) "Data on participation", which provides the numbers and percentages of women;

(c) "Discussion", which identifies overall trends, looks at the number of women in important posts, ranks the bodies according to their political significance and discloses issue-to-issue variations in participation.

In the subsections that provide the data, the bodies are grouped according to the issue they deal with, that is, defence, disarmament, foreign affairs or foreign aid. Bodies dealing with these four issues, and sometimes with all other issues as well, are presented together and called general-issue bodies. At the end of each subsection, female representation in bodies responsible for defence, disarmament, foreign affairs and foreign aid is compared with female representation in bodies dealing with other issues. The reader is directed to the appropriate appendix tables by cross-references.*

The Swedish names of the authorities, ministerial committees and titles were translated by the Translation Section of the Ministry for Foreign Affairs.

D. Equal representation

In Sweden, the term "equal opportunity" is normally applied in the context of the two sexes. It refers to the concept that women and men should have equal rights, obligations and opportunities to hold jobs that make them financially independent, to care for children and for their homes and to participate in political and social life. 1/

"Equality" is a broader concept than equal opportunity. It applies to relations between all individuals and social groups and is based on the belief that people are of equal value irrespective of sex, race, religion or social class. Equal opportunity is one of the elements of equality and a very important one. 2/ In this report, the percentages and numbers of women will be studied.

Very briefly, equal opportunity developed as follows in Sweden: in 1846, widows, divorced women and unmarried women became entitled to work in manual trades and some sectors of commerce. Between 1866 and 1921, only men with a certain income and status had the right to vote, but since 1921 suffrage has been universal for adults. In that same year, 1921, the first woman was elected to the Swedish Riksdag, and in 1947 the first woman was appointed a Cabinet minister. Today the right to vote is used fully: 93 per cent of all women and 92 per cent of all men between the ages of 18 and 74 voted in the 1985 election. 3/ The number of members in the Riksdag is now (1987) 349,** of whom 113, or 32 per cent, are women.

---

*Appendices 1-3 are contained in the annex.

**The Riksdag changed from two chambers to one in 1971. Before 1971, the number of members was 151 in the first chamber and 233 in the second chamber, a total of 384 members. Between 1971 and 1976, the total number of members of the Riksdag was 350; after 1976, this changed to 349.

In 1974, parental leave was introduced, entitling either the mother or the father to a paid leave of absence after the birth of a child. An equal opportunity agreement between employers and unions was reached in 1977 and again in 1983. In 1983 all occupational categories were also opened for women, including the armed forces. The following year an equal opportunity agreement was signed for the civil service. 4/

There exists a goal* within the decision-making bodies of Sweden that the proportion of women should not be less than 40 per cent, which according to the Central Services Office for the Ministries is an accepted norm. 5/

*Since the present report was written, this goal has been explicitly stated in Swedish Governmental Bill 1987/88:105. The goal remains 40 per cent for all employees but has been raised to 50 per cent, by 1999, in the case of boards of central government authorities.

I. THE SWEDISH POLITICAL SYSTEM 1967-1987: WOMEN'S REPRESENTATION ANALYSED

A. Women in decision-making bodies within the Riksdag

1. Bodies examined

In this section, the following bodies are examined: (a) the Riksdag as a whole, (b) the Advisory Council on Foreign Affairs, (c) the War Delegation, (d) the Swedish Delegation to the Nordic Council, (e) the Executive Committee of the Riksdag Interparliamentary Group, (f) the Standing Committee on Defence and (g) the Standing Committee on Foreign Affairs.*

The Riksdag as a whole and four of the other decision-making bodies, that is, bodies (b) through (e), are general-issue bodies. They deal with all the issues with which we are concerned. The standing committees on defence and foreign affairs deal exclusively with defence and with foreign affairs and foreign aid respectively.

All members of the Riksdag are elected simultaneously through free, secret and direct elections, every third year. The Riksdag receives Government proposals in the form of bills (propositioner) and private member proposals, or motions (motioner).** These bills and motions are discussed in the 16 standing committees*** (utskott) of the Riksdag. Since 1 January 1988, the meetings of a standing committee can be opened to the public if the majority of the members of the committee so decides. In previous years, however, the meetings of the committees were not public; only their reports were published. Their members are appointed exclusively from, and by, the Riksdag members (no Cabinet ministers may be appointed, however) on the basis of party strength. No Cabinet ministers may be appointed, however. The committees have 15 permanent members (ledamöter) and at least 15 deputy members (suppleanter). All members of the Riksdag except Cabinet ministers (who can also be members of the Riksdag) are appointed to be permanent or deputy members of the standing committees. They can be appointed to more than one committee. Substitutes take over the duties of the Cabinet ministers and the Speaker of the Riksdag.

All the committees have secretaries who are responsible for the day-to-day of the Committee. A secretary (kanslichef) is the head of the secretariat and thus holds a strategic position.

_____

*The Advisory Council on Foreign Affairs, the War Delegation and the two standing committees are decision-making bodies within the Riksdag (Riksdagensorgan), while the Swedish Delegation to the Nordic Council is one of the five governmental authorities subordinated to the Riksdag (Riksdagensmyndigheter). The Executive Committee of the Riksdag Interparliamentary Group is the special body for members of the Riksdag (see Fakta om Folkvalda: Riksdagen 1985-1988 (Stockholm, Central Services Office for Parliament, 1986), pp. 9-11).

**Motions can be written by one or more members of the Riksdag, ranging from one political party to all. This is an important opportunity to influence decisions made by the Government.

***The number of committees increased during the period 1967-1987 (see appendix 1, table 1).

The Advisory Council on Foreign Affairs (Utrikesnämnden), established in 1921, consists of the Head of State (the King), who is the Chairperson, the Speaker of the Riksdag and nine other Riksdag members. The latter are elected by the Riksdag, and the period for which they are elected is the same as that of the Riksdag. The Advisory Council deliberates with the Government on important matters of foreign affairs. 6/

In case of war or danger of war, the War Delegation (Krigsdelegationen) replaces the Riksdag and takes over its duties. The Delegation is established within the Riksdag and consists of the Speaker of the Riksdag, who is its Chairperson, and 50 other members. Only permanent Riksdag members can be appointed. They are elected by the Riksdag for the period of the Riksdag. The War Delegation is appointed on the basis of party strength in the ordinary Riksdag and is thus a Riksdag in miniature. 7/

The Nordic Council, established in 1952, is a body consisting of parliamentarians from the five Nordic countries that gives recommendations to the Governments of these countries. 8/ Each Government appoints a special minister responsible for the co-ordination of Nordic affairs and together the special ministers comprise the Nordic Council of Ministers. 9/ The Swedish Delegation to the Nordic Council consists of about 20 members* who are elected from the Riksdag.

The Riksdag Interparliamentary Group entered the Interparliamentary Union in 1892. The Executive Committee of the Riksdag Interparliamentary Group is the decision-making body of this group; its delegates have a representative function. The aim is to promote personal contacts among parliamentarians and to develop parliamentarism and work for peace and international co-operation. 10/

The political importance of these seven decision-making bodies differs. The Riksdag as a whole is formally the most important, because it decides on all bills and motions. The bills and motions are discussed in the standing committees, which give their recommendations on how to make decisions. As the strength of the parties is the same in these committees as in the Riksdag as a whole, their recommendations are nearly always followed by the Riksdag. Consequently, the work in these committees is very important.

The Advisory Council is not formally a decision-making body, but it is regarded as politically important. Government as well as opposition is represented, including the relevant Cabinet ministers, party leaders and some chairpersons of the standing committees, and Swedish foreign affairs are discussed, under the leadership of the King.

In peacetime the War Delegation has no political function at all, but it is potentially important as it takes over the duties of the Riksdag as a whole in case of war or danger of war.

2. Data on representation

General-issue bodies

An analysis follows of the participation of women in the Riksdag as a whole, the Advisory Council, the War Delegation, the Swedish Delegation to the Nordic Council, the Executive Committee of the Riksdag Interparliamentary

---

*The number of delegates has changed (see appendix 1, table 4).

Group (appendix 1, tables A1.1-A1.5) and the political parties. If both permanent and deputy members* are counted, it is evident that the percentage of women in these five authorities increased between 1966/67 and 1986/87. The participation of women in the Riksdag increased steadily, from 13 per cent in both chambers in 1966/67 to 32 per cent in 1986/87. Female representation in the Council and the War Delegation was lower than in the Riksdag as a whole in 1986/87, but it was higher in the Swedish Delegation and the Executive Committee.

Focusing on permanent and deputy members separately (see tables 5 and 6 in appendix 1), it can be seen that the proportion of female permanent members in all five bodies increased, but not very fast. The exception is the Executive Committee. In 1976/77, 56 per cent of its permanent members were women, but this proportion decreased to 22 per cent in 1986/87. The proportion of female deputy members in this body increased during the same period, from 14 per cent to 57 per cent. In the Swedish Delegation and the Advisory Council, the representation of female deputy members has varied, and in 1986/87 there was a large difference between the two bodies: 45 per cent of the deputy members in the Swedish Delegation were women in that year, while the corresponding figure for the Council was 17 per cent.

The Speaker of the Riksdag has always been a man. One woman was a deputy speaker in 1986/87, the First Deputy Speaker.** Since the speaker of the Riksdag is automatically Chairperson of the War Delegation, the latter post was filled by a man during each of the three years in question. The same condition prevailed in the Advisory Council: the Head of State, the King, is Chairperson. In the Swedish Delegation to the Nordic Council, both the Chairperson and the Deputy Chairperson were women in 1986/87. Previously these posts had been held by men. In the Executive Committee of the Riksdag Interparliamentary Group, the posts of Chairperson and Deputy Chairperson have always been held by men except in 1986/87, when the Deputy Chairperson was a woman.

When the data for the Riksdag are broken down by political party, i.e., the Moderate Party, the Centre Party, the Liberal Party, the Swedish Social Democratic Party and the Left Party Communists,*** it can be seen that female participation varied somewhat, both within a party for each of the three years and between the five parties (table 1). The Liberal Party had the highest female representation in 1986/87.

_____

*The Riksdag as a whole and the War Delegation have permanent members only (see appendix 1, tables 4-6).

**There are three deputy speakers of the Riksdag. All four speakers of the Riksdag are elected for the election period of the Riksdag, that is, three years.

***The political parties are here ranked from right to left in political sympathy, with the Moderate Party regarded as conservative. The Centre Party is mostly an agrarian party. In 1966/67, the Swedish name for the Moderate Party was Riksdagshögern and the Left Party Communists were called Kommunisterna.

Table 1. Female participation in each of the five political
parties within the Riksdag, 1966/67, 1976/77 and
1986/87

| Political party | Per cent (number) of women in each party | | |
	1966/67 a/	1976/77	1986/87
Moderate	14(8)	16(9)	25(19)
Centre	2(1)	28(24)	38(17)
Liberal	7(5)	23(9)	41(21)
Social Democratic	18(35)	22(34)	33(53)
Left Party Communists	11(1)	24(4)	16(3)
All parties b/	13(50)	23(80)	32(113)
Number of Riksdag members	384	349	349

Sources: Riksdagsmatrikel 1967 (Stockholm, Kungliga Boktryckeriet, 1967),
Part I, p. 30 and Part II, p. 43; Riksdagsmatrikel 1976/77 (Stockholm, Central
Services Office for Parliament, 1977), Part I, p. 78; and Sveriges Riksdag
1986/87 (Stockholm, Central Services Office for Parliament, 1986), p. 8.

a/ The figures are for both chambers (see appendix 1, table 3, for
information about each chamber).

b/ A party called Medborgerlig Samling had one member, a man, in the
second chamber in 1966/67.

Defence-issue body

Defence issues in the Riksdag are dealt with mainly by the Standing Committee on Defence. This committee did not exist in 1966/67, so the figures
presented for that year refer to the Standing Committee of Supply/1st Division
(see appendix 1, table B1.1). Since the members of the standing committees
are appointed on the basis of the parties' strength in the Riksdag, their
female/male proportions may be compared with that of the Riksdag as a whole.

The Standing Committee on Defence has a smaller proportion of women than
the Riksdag. Only in 1966/67 was the share of female permanent members higher
in the Committee than in the Riksdag as a whole, but this is because at that
time there were only six permanent members in the Committee, one of them a
woman. In 1976/77 and 1986/87, by contrast, the total number of permanent
members was 15, two and three of them (13 per cent and 20 per cent), respectively, being women. The Chairperson and the Deputy Chairperson were men in
all three years.

Except for 1966/67, the number of female deputy members was higher than
the number of female permanent members. In 1966/67 there were no female
deputy members, in 1976/77 there were three and in 1986/87 there were six.*
In all three years, the Secretary of the Committee was a man.

---

*The number of deputy members was different in all three years. There
were 12 deputy members in 1966/67 and 16 and 19 deputy members in 1976/77 and
1986/87, respectively (see appendix 1, table B1.1b).

It can be seen that the proportion of female members, both permanent and deputy, of the Standing Committee on Defence has been quite low. Overall, however, the representation of women increased from 1966/67 to 1988/87.

Foreign affairs/foreign aid-issue body

The decision-making body of the Riksdag that is responsible in matters of foreign affairs and foreign aid is the Standing Committee on Foreign Affairs (appendix 1, table D1.1). The permanent members of this Committee are compared with the Riksdag as a whole.

The percentage of female permanent members of the Standing Committee on Foreign Affairs varied over the three years. The number of permanent members also changed: 16 in 1966/67 and 15 in 1976/77 and 1986/87). In 1966/67 the Committee had a smaller percentage of female permanent members (6 per cent) than the Riksdag as a whole, while in the other two years it had a slightly greater percentage (33 per cent).

The data for deputy members are somewhat different than those for permanent members. In both 1966/67 and 1976/77, female deputy members made up 12 per cent of the membership. The corresponding figure for 1986/87 was 33 per cent. This means that since 1976/77 the percentage of female permanent members stayed the same, while the percentage of female deputy members increased, so that in 1986/87 the percentage of permanent and deputy women members was the same.

In all three years, the post of Chairperson was held by men. A woman held the post of Deputy Chairperson both in 1976/77 and 1986/87. At all three times the Secretary was a man.

Comparison with all standing committees (1986)

To enable a comparison to be made between female representation in bodies dealing with defence, disarmament, foreign affairs and foreign aid and female representation in bodies dealing with other issues, all 16 standing committees of the Riksdag were studied. Female representation among the permanent members of all 16 committees was 28 per cent in March 1986. Of the 16 chairpersons, 3 were women and of the deputy chairpersons 2 were women. Committees dealing with cultural and social issues had a majority of women; the other committees were dominated by men (table 2). In the Standing Committee on Social Questions and the 55anding Committee on Social Insurance, these secretaries were women. The remaining 14 secretaries were men. 11/

Table 2. Male and female permanent and deputy members
in the 16 standing committees of the Swedish
Riksdag, March 1986 a/
(Percentage)

Standing committee b/	Permanent members		Deputy members	
	Women	Men	Women	Men
Cultural Affairs	60 c/, d/	40	44	56
Social Insurance	60 c/	40	60	40

continued

Table 2 (continued)

Standing committee b/	Permanent members		Deputy members	
	Women	Men	Women	Men
Social Questions	47	53	50	50
Civil Law Legislation	33	67	47	53
Justice	27 c/	73	33	67
Foreign Affairs	27 d/	73	35	65
Labour Market	27	73	30	70
Education	27	73	41	59
Housing	20	80	31	69
Finance	20	80	33	67
Defence	20	80	33	67
Agriculture	20	80	11	89
Constitution	20	80	50	50
Industry and Commerce	20	80	21	79
Taxation	13	87	29	71
Transport and Communications	13	87	33	67
Average	28	72	36	64

Source: Central Services Office for Parliament, Fakta om Folkvalda: Riksdagen 1985-1988 (Stockholm, Central Services Office for Parliament, 1986), pp. 325-332.

a/ The number of permanent members is always 15.

b/ Ranked by percentage of female permanent members.

c/ The Chairperson is a woman.

d/ The Deputy Chairperson is a woman.

3. Discussion

Overall trend

All seven decision-making bodies were analysed to see if a trend could be discerned. If both permanent and deputy members were counted, the trend in all the bodies was an increase in female representation. The representation of women within the Riksdag as a whole increased steadily, as did their representation within each of the five political parties within the Riksdag. Only the Swedish Delegation to the Nordic Council achieved female participation of 40 per cent in 1986/87; in all three years, the other units had a female participation that was lower, or much lower, than 40 per cent (table 3).*

---

*The 40 per cent figure corresponds to the goal set by and for Swedish decision-making bodies (see introduction, section D).

Table 3. Female representation, both permanent and deputy,
in seven decision-making bodies in the Riksdag
(Percentage)

Decision-making body	1966/67	1976/77	1986/87
Riksdag as a whole a/	13	23	32
Advisory Council on Foreign Affairs	9	13	17
War Delegation a/	12	12	18
Swedish Delegation to the Nordic Council	12	25	40
Executive Committee of the Riksdag Interparliamentary Group	13	38	38
Standing Committee on Defence	6	16	26
Standing Committee on Foreign Affairs	9	23	33

Source: Appendix 1, tables A1.1–A1.5, B1.1 and D1.1.

a/ The Riksdag and the War Delegation have only permanent members.

Participation in important posts

Which positions within these decision-making bodies are normally held, or not held, by women? Has the picture changed over the period? An examination of the seven bodies shows that there were few female chairpersons or deputy chairpersons. Of 22 chairpersons, 1 was a woman as were 5 out of 30 deputy chairpersons.* Taking all 16 standing committees into consideration, the same picture prevails (appendix 1, table 1).

Why is the representation so low? The interviewees gave some additional information. The principle of appointing by seniority, that is, by number of working years in the Riksdag, seems to be an important factor. Only recently has a relatively high proportion of parliamentarians been women, so not many of them have yet acquired the needed seniority. This implies that only persons with a great number of working years in the Riksdag become chairpersons and deputy chairpersons of the standing committees. Examining the number of years the persons who held these posts after the 1985 election had been members of the Riksdag when they were appointed to the posts, the average number of years needed to get the posts can be determined (table 4). As seen in the table, it seems that women need more years than men to get a post as chairperson but

---

*Chairpersons: in 1966/67, two speakers of the Riksdag (one in each chamber), and in 1976/77 and 1986/87 one speaker of the Riksdag each year, for a subtotal of four. One chairperson in each of the two standing committees each year, a subtotal of six. One chairperson in the other four decision-making bodies each year, a subtotal of 12. Altogether, therefore, 22 chairpersons (4 + 6 + 12). Deputy chairpersons: in 1966/67, six deputy speakers (three in each chamber), in 1976/77 and 1986/87 three deputy speakers each year, for a subtotal of 12. One deputy chairperson in each of the two standing committees each year, a subtotal of six. One deputy chairperson in each of the other four decision-making bodies each year, a subtotal of 12. Altogether, therefore, 30 deputy chairpersons (12 + 6 + 12).

fewer years than men to get a post as deputy chairperson. If we take into account both posts, they need, on average, fewer years than men. This could mean that seniority is more important when appointing chairpersons than when appointing deputy chairpersons.

Table 4. Chairpersons and deputy chairpersons in the 16 standing committees after the 1985 election: average number of years as members of the Riksdag before being appointed as chairperson or deputy chairperson of the standing committee, by sex

Position	Average number of years a/		
	Men	Women	Both
Chairpersons	12.6	14.0	12.9
Deputy chairpersons	12.9	8.5	10.1
Both chairpersons and deputy chairpersons	12.7	11.8	12.6

Source: Fakta om Folkvalda: Riksdagen 1985-1988 (Stockholm, Central Services Office for Parliament, 1986), pp. 15-306 and 325-332.

a/ Calculation: the year when the person who in 1985 was either chairperson or deputy chairperson was appointed, minus the year when the person was elected member of the Riksdag, is equal to the number of years as a member before getting the post of either chairperson or deputy chairperson. For example, the total number of years for all 32 chairpersons and deputy chairpersons was 403 (403/32 = 12.6 years, on average). Number of women: 5 (3 chairpersons and 2 deputy chairpersons). Number of men: 27.

When the 20-year span is looked at as a whole, it can be seen that the number of female chairpersons and deputy chairpersons increased. In 1966/67 there were no female chairpersons or deputy chairpersons in the seven bodies examined here. Of the chairpersons in the 10 standing committees (see appendix 1, table 1a), two were women, but there were no female deputy chairpersons. In 1986/87 there was one female chairperson and four female deputy chairpersons, including the First Deputy Speaker of the Riksdag, in the seven bodies. In all the 16 standing committees, three chairpersons and two deputy chairpersons were women, one of them in the Standing Committee on Foreign Affairs.

The difference in female participation between permanent members and deputy members is not clear. The difference between decision-making bodies is great, however, both with regard to development over the period and to differences between the two categories of members each year. It may be insufficient to study only 3 years out of a period of 20 years to be able to draw firm conclusions on this point. Further research is necessary.

For instance, in 1986/87 five of the seven decision-making bodies* had one common feature: female representation among permanent members was lower

_____

*All but the Riksdag as a whole or the War Delegation, because the data for these two bodies include only permanent members.

than or equal to* female representation among deputy members. In the other two years the picture was different. In two and three of these bodies, in 1966/67 and 1976/77, respectively, the female representation was lower among deputy members than among permanent members.** Thus it cannot in general be said that the share of women tends to be higher among deputy members than among permanent members.

Some of the interviewees also claimed that the average female member of the Riksdag probably had more appointments than the average male member. This claim can be tested by examining appointments to the 16 standing committees. Every member of the Riksdag, except those who are Cabinet ministers, is appointed a permanent or deputy member in at least one of the 16 standing committees. In 1986 there were 113 women in the Riksdag and 236 men. The total number of appointments to the committee was 515 (appendix 1, tables 2a-b). This gives an average of 1.48 appointments for each member (table 5). If we make the same calculations for women and men separately, we get 1.47 for men and 1.48 for women, which is not a significant difference.

Focusing on permanent and deputy members separately, the following picture emerges. For men only, the average number of appointments as permanent member is 0.73 and as deputy member, 0.75. The corresponding figures for women parliamentarians are 0.60 and 0.88. This means that women are more often appointed as deputy members than as permanent members, if all 16 standing committees are taken into account.***

The two standing committees, defence and foreign affairs, that have been studied in each of the three years rather than only in 1986 can be examined to see if the same picture emerges. Female representation with regard to permanent and deputy members in these two committees changed over the 20-year period. In the foreign affairs committee, female participation in 1966/67 was higher among deputy members than among permanent members. In 1976/77 it was the other way round, and in 1986/87 the two categories had the same percentage of women.

In the defence committee, the development has been different. In 1966/67 there was a higher percentage of women among the permanent members, while in both other years the proportion of females among permanent members was lower than among deputy members. It seems to have been more common in later years to appoint women as deputy members than as permanent members. To see if this general pattern holds for all 16 standing committees, more research has to be carried out.

---

*In the Advisory Council on Foreign Affairs, there were two women in both categories; however, because there was one person more among deputy members, the proportion of female members was only 17 per cent compared to 18 per cent among permanent members.

**It is interesting to note that the two bodies that had had a higher percentage of female permanent members than deputy members in 1966/67 experienced a reversal of this situation in 1976/77, while the three bodies that had had a lower percentage of female permanent members than deputy members in 1966/67 also experienced a reversal in 1976/77.

***The same phenomenon was also seen in previous years (see e.g. Steg på väg - Natdnell Handlingsplan för jämställhet utarbetad av jämställhetnommiden (Sou 1979:5b, p 103).

Table 5. Average number of appointments as member, permanent and deputy,
of the 16 standing committees, by sex, March 1986

Number of members of the Riksdag	Number of members of the standing committees			Average number of appointments as		
	Permanent	Deputy	Both	Permanent a/	Deputy a/	Both b/
Women	113	68	99	167	0.60	0.88	1.48
Men	236	172	176	348	0.73	0.75	1.47
Total	349	240	275	515	0.69	0.79	1.48

Source: Appendix 1, table 2.

a/ Total number of permanent members (PM) = 172 (men) + 68 (women) = 240.
Total number of deputy members (DM) = 176 (men) + 99 (women) = 275. Total
number of female members of the Riksdag (MoR) = 113. Total number of male
MoR = 236.

240 PM/349 MoR = 0.69 appointments (app.) as PM for one MoR

275 DM/349 MoR = 0.79 app. as DM for one MoR

172 male PM/236 male MoR = 0.73 app. as PM for a male MoR

176 male DM/236 male MoR = 0.75 app. as DM for a male MoR

68 female PM/113 female MoR = 0.60 app. as PM for female MoR

99 female DM/113 female MoR = 0.88 app. as DM for a female MoR

b/ The 348 male members of the committees are broken down into 172 permanent members and 176 deputy members. The 167 female members of the committees are broken down into 68 permanent members and 99 deputy members. This
gives us a total of 515 (348 + 167) appointments to the committees divided by
349 members of the Riksdag = 1.48 appointments per member of the Riksdag.
Furthermore, 348 male members of the 16 standing committees/236 male members
of the Riksdag = 1.47 appointments/male member of the Riksdag; 167 female
members of the committees/113 female members of the Riksdag = 1.48
appointments/female member of the Riksdag.

When female participation in the standing committees on defence and
foreign affairs is compared with their participation in the 14 other standing
committees (appendix 1, tables 2a-b), the first two are roughly in the middle
of the rankings with regard to permanent members and deputy members. In the
majority of committees, female representation is between 20 and 40 per cent
among both permanent and deputy members; some, however, have a female participation of greater than 40 per cent and others have a participation of less
than 20 per cent. It can be seen that the difference between permanent and
deputy members is large. Six of the 16 committees have a female participation
of greater than 40 per cent if only deputy members are counted, but only three
of the committees have a female participation of greater than 40 per cent if
permanent members are counted.

Bodies ranked by political importance

Is the participation of women high or low in politically important
decision-making bodies? In the Riksdag the participation of women rose

steadily during the period. The Advisory Council on Foreign Affairs and the War Delegation, the first of which is important and the second, potentially important, are far from having as much female representation as the Riksdag. The gap was especially pronounced in 1986/87 (see table 3). In that year, two bodies of lesser political importance, the Swedish Delegation to the Nordic Council and the Executive Committee of the Riksdag Interparliamentary Group, had the highest participation of women. Although the number of cases may be too small to allow a general conclusion, it is interesting to examine these four decision-making bodies more closely.*

Female participation in the War Delegation, which is a miniature Riksdag, is very low; however, this body is not politically important in peacetime. In 1966/67 and 1976/77 only 6 of the 51 members were women; in 1986/87, the figure was 9. Closer examination reveals that its members are the chair-persons and deputy chairpersons of the 16 standing committees, the leaders and deputy leaders of the political parties, the Cabinet ministers and other important persons in each of the political parties. Since, as we have seen, there are not many women in the latter posts, there are few women in the War Delegation. The composition of the Advisory Council is similar in this respect, which means that the participation of women is low. Few women are included in these two bodies where the parties place important representatives.

The Executive Committee, a less important authority politically speaking, had a higher proportion of women than the Riksdag in 1976/77, when over half the permanent members of the former were women. It is an exception to the overall pattern of low female participation. Why its female participation has declined since then is a question that needs to be explored in further research. Another politically less important body, the Swedish Delegation, also had a greater proportion of female permanent members, 35 per cent, than the Riksdag, but this was in 1986/87.

Thus, even if the sample is too small to permit general conclusions, it is clear that in the politically important body, the Advisory Council,** and the potentially important body, the War Delegation, the participation of women was lower than in the Riksdag as a whole in all three years. On the other hand, in the two other bodies, which might be regarded as having less political importance, female participation is equal to or greater than in the Riksdag as a whole. Of the seven decision-making bodies being covered (see table 3), the Riksdag as a whole, formally the most important body, was in fourth place in 1986/87 with respect to female representation.

The two standing committees are, strictly speaking, equally important. However, some of the interviewees pointed out that an informal ranking might give the foreign affairs committee more importance than the defence committee. In both, the participation of women rose over the 20-year period, in the Standing Committee on Foreign Affairs a little more than in the Standing Committee on Defence. Except in 1966/67, the former had the highest female participation. Thus, in this case, the more important body had the higher proportion of women.

---

*The members of all seven decision-making bodies, except the Riksdag as a whole, are nominated by the executive committees of the political parties.

**Not formally a decision-making body; its function was discussed earlier in this chapter.

Issue-specific differences in participation

In which issues is the representation of women high and in which is it low? The only clear difference is the one between the standing committees for foreign affairs and defence, which suggests that there may be greater repre-sentation of females in bodies dealing with foreign affairs and foreign aid than in bodies dealing with defence issues.

B. Women in decision-making bodies within the Swedish Government and the Government Office and within ministerial committees

In this section will be analysed the representation of women in two cate-gories of bodies: (a) the Government as a whole and the Government Office and (b) some ministerial committees set up by the Ministry of Defence and the Ministry for Foreign Affairs.

1. The Government and the Government Office

Bodies examined

The Government as a whole, the Office of the Prime Minister, the Ministry of Defence and the Ministry for Foreign Affairs are included here. At this time, 1987, there are 20 Cabinet ministers (statsrad). Thirteen of them are in charge of ministries (departementschefer);* the other seven are known as consultative ministers (konsultativa statsrad), or ministers without portfolio. The Prime Minister belongs to the latter group, although he is the most impor-tant minister. However, in this study the post of Prime Minister is treated as a separate category. The remaining ministers without portfolio are generally responsible for special spheres of activities within the ministries. The Government is collectively responsible for all decisions. 12/

The ministries are, together with the Office of the Prime Minister (Statsradsberedningen), collectively known as the Government Office. The primary task of the Office of the Prime Minister is to co-ordinate the work of the thirteen ministries, but it is also a politically important body as it has a policy-making function. 13/

The Government as a whole is the most important of the four decision-making bodies included in this chapter. The two ministries are equally impor-tant, but less important than the Government as a whole. The Office of the Prime Minister is important as well, but it has a different role from the others.

Within the Ministry for Foreign Affairs, the department that deals exclusively with disarmament issues can be singled out: the Swedish Disarma-ment Commission (Nedrustningsdelegationen inom UD). The Ambassador of Disarmament is head of the Disarmament Commission and also the Chairperson of the Delegation of Disarmament (Nedrustningsdelegationen, den parlamentariskt sammansatta) (see also chapter I.C.1).

As the focus is on decision-making persons, only top officials, advisers and officials responsible for processing issues (handläggare) are examined.

_____

*The number of Cabinet ministers and ministries changed from 1966/67 to 1986/87 (see appendix 2A for further information).

Data on representation

General-issue bodies

Focusing on the participation of women in the Government as a whole, as well as on the Office of the Prime Minister (see appendix 2A, tables 2, 3, A2.1 and A2.2), it can be seen that in 1976/77 and 1986/87 the total number of Cabinet ministers in the Government was 20, five of whom were women. In 1966/67 two of the 17 Cabinet ministers were women. In all three years, the women have, with one exception, been ministers without portfolio or heads of ministries dealing with the labour market, housing or social issues. The exception was in 1976/77, when a woman was the Minister for Foreign Affairs.

In 1986/87 female consultative ministers had special responsibility for equal opportunities and immigration, energy and environmental issues and issues concerning international aid. 14/

Within the Office of the Prime Minister the participation of women increased steadily over the time period examined in this study. In 1966/67 there were no female officials in the Office; in 1986/87 there were slightly more than 40 per cent.

In the Office of the Prime Minister three categories of employee have been examined: head officials, advisers (political, legal and special) and officials responsible for processing issues. Within the first category there were two women out of seven in 1986/87; the other two years no women held such positions. The second and third categories had rather high percentages of women, between 30 and 50 per cent, both in 1976/77 and 1986/87. In 1966/67 no advisers were employed and there were no female officials with responsibility for processing issues.

Defence-issue body

The Ministry of Defence has generally had a low proportion of female employees. In 1966/67 there was only 1 woman in the categories here examined, in 1976/77 there were 6 and in 1986/87, 13 (appendix 2A, table B2.1). It can be seen that only in 1976/77 did women hold posts as head officials (12 per cent). Both women were deputy assistant under-secretaries, one of the lower categories among the head officials. In the other two categories examined here, advisers and officials responsible for processing issues, the second category is the one in which female participation is highest. In 1966/67 there were no female advisers, in the other two years there was one woman. In the last category the number of women was one, three and twelve, respectively (5, 9 and 24 per cent in the three years).

Foreign affairs/foreign aid-issue body

The total number of employees in the Ministry for Foreign Affairs increased considerably during the period. In the three categories examined, the total rose from 78 persons in 1966/67 to 330 in 1986/87. Also, the percentage of women increased, from 4 per cent in 1966/67 to 11 per cent in 1976/77 and, finally, to 33 per cent in 1986/87 (appendix 2A, table D2.1). Thus, as the total number of employees rose, the percentage of female officials also increased. The largest increase was among officials with responsibility for processing issues. In 1986/87, the proportion of women in this category was almost 44 per cent.

The Swedish Disarmament Commission is a department within the Ministry for Foreign Affairs, not a separate body. According to the Ambassador of Disarmament, who is the head of this department, the position has always been held by a woman.

Comparison with all head officials (1986)

To enable a comparison to be made between female representation in bodies dealing only with defence, disarmament, foreign affairs and foreign aid and female representation in bodies dealing with other issues, head officials within the Government Office as a whole have also been studied. The representation of women among the head officials in the Government Office was about 10 per cent in March 1986 (table 6).

Table 6. Head officials in the Government Office
by position and sex, 1 March 1986

Position	Women	Men
Under-Secretary of State	2	25
Permanent Under-Secretary of State	4	10
Under-Secretary for Legal Affairs	–	14
Head of Planning	–	5
Head of Budget	–	1
Political Chief Official	–	1
Under-Secretary of State for Foreign Affairs	–	1
Total	6	57
	9.5%	90.5%

Source: Statistics Sweden (SCB), Kvinnooch Mansvär(1)den: Fakta om jämställdheten: Sverige 1986 (Stockholm, Norstedts Tryckeri, 1986).

According to a report 15/ on equal opportunities within the Government Office, 3,150 officials were employed by the Government Office in July 1986. This includes 12 ministries, the Office of the Prime Minister and the Central Services Office for the Ministries (Regeringskansliets förvaltningskontor). The thirteenth Ministry was established in 1987. Of these officials, 58 per cent were women. Not including the Ministry for Foreign Affairs,* the number of women was 963, or 61 per cent (appendix 2A, table 1).

_____

*Altogether 1,571 persons were employed at the Ministry for Foreign Affairs in 1987, of whom about 940 were stationed at Stockholm, the rest abroad at embassies, delegations and consulates (The Ministry for Foreign Affairs, Data över könsfördelningen bland de anställda vid Utrikesdepartementet, 1987).

Focusing on head officials* and officials with responsibility for processing issues, the figures become somewhat different: 30 per cent of these were women. Not including the Ministry for Foreign Affairs, the corresponding figure was 36 per cent. The report concludes that women dominate the lower echelons of employees and men, the higher. 16/

Discussion

Overall trend

The following analysis of these four decision-making bodies makes clear the trend. If the three categories of officials, that is, head officials, advisers and officials responsible for processing issues, are counted together, the participation of women has increased steadily in all four decision-making bodies. All four had their lowest proportion of women in 1966/67 and their highest in 1986/87. The Office of the Prime Minister had a representation of women greater than 40 per cent in 1986/87, while the other three bodies had representations between 16 and 33 per cent (table 7).

Table 7. Female representation in four decision-making
bodies within the Government Office
(Percentage)

Decision-making body	1966/67	1976/77	1986/87
Government as a whole	12	25	25
Office of the Prime Minister	0	26	41
Ministry of Defence	2	9	16
Ministry for Foreign Affairs	4	11	33

Source: Appendix 2A, tables A2.1, A2.2, B2.1, D2.1.

Participation in important posts

Which positions are normally held, or not held, by women in these four decision-making bodies? Has the picture changed over the period? Concentrating for the moment on the Government, it is evident that ministers with responsibility for a ministry are considered more important than consultative ministers. To see if there is any significant difference between these two groups with respect to women's participation, the percentage of female Cabinet ministers responsible for a ministry and the percentage of female consultative ministers have been calculated (table 8).

_____

*According to the source: not including head officials in ministerial committees (see chapter I.B.2), Cabinet ministers, under-secretaries of state, legal advisers or political advisers (see also appendix 2A, table 1).

Table 8. Female Cabinet ministers responsible for a ministry and
female consultative ministers, 1966/67, 1976/77 and
1986/87

Year	Cabinet ministers responsible for a ministry			Consultative ministers			All ministers, including the Prime Minister a/		
	Total	Women	% Women	Total	Women	% Women	Total	Women	% Women
1966/67	11	0	0	5	2	40	17	2	12
1976/77	14	2	14	5	3	60	20	5	25
1986/87	12	2	17	7	3	43	20	5	25

Sources: Sveriges Statskalender 1967 (Uppsala, Almqvist and Wiksells, 1967), p. 57; Sveriges Statskalender 1977 (Stockholm, Liber Allmänna Förlaget, 1977), p. 43; Sveriges Statskalender 1986 (Stockholm, Liber Allmänna Förlaget, 1986), p. 55.

a/ The Prime Minister was a male in all three years.

It can be seen that women are more often appointed as consultative ministers than as Cabinet ministers responsible for a ministry. The Prime Minister was a man during all three years; indeed, no woman has ever been Prime Minister in Sweden.

To confirm this finding, we can look at all Cabinet ministers by position during the period 1969-1986. There were 118 Cabinet ministers, including prime ministers, Cabinet ministers with responsibility for a ministry and consultative ministers during that period. Of all Cabinet ministers, 25, or 21 per cent, have been women. Among the 81 ministers with responsibility for a ministry, there were 8 women, or 10 per cent. The number of female consultative ministers during the period was considerably higher: 17 of the 31 ministers in this group were women, that is, 55 per cent. As stated above, there has not been any female prime minister, out of six altogether. 17/

Furthermore, the eight women responsible for ministries were all appointed since 1976. Before that year, no woman had held that position. Among consultative ministers, on the other hand, there were women the whole time, from 1969 to 1986.*

An examination of the three other decision-making bodies being studied here shows that, with a few exceptions, the lowest percentage of women was among the top officials and the highest percentage was among officials with responsibility for processing issues. The exception to this overall situation was in 1967/77, when the Minister for Foreign Affairs was a woman. There has also been a slight increase in representation among top officials, but it has not been as pronounced as in representation among advisers and the officials responsible for processing an issue.

---

*The calculation is done for the period 1969-1986. Notice, however, that the first woman was appointed Cabinet minister, without portfolio, in 1947. In 1951 a woman was appointed Cabinet minister with responsibility for Ecclesiastical Affairs. During the period 1951-1969 four women held posts as Cabinet ministers without portfolio.

In summary, the women in the four decision-making bodies discussed in this chapter did not generally hold positions at the top of the hierarchy. There was, however, some progress in the direction of equal representation during the period.

Bodies ranked by political importance

Do women participate substantially in politically important decision-making bodies? As already mentioned, the Government is considered to be the most important body, followed by the two ministries and the Office of the Prime Minister.

Looking at figures for 1986/87 for the three categories of officials, these bodies can be ranked with respect to the participation of women, from highest to lowest: the Office of the Prime Minister, the Ministry for Foreign Affairs, the Government as a whole and the Ministry of Defence (see table 7). In 1966/67 the picture was totally different. At that time the Government had the highest proportion of women, followed by the Ministry for Foreign Affairs, the Ministry of Defence and, finally, the Office of the Prime Minister.

Even though the participation of women in all four decision-making bodies increased during the period, the most important body, the Government, dropped from first to third place. Furthermore, in that body the participation of women had not increased by 1986/87, although during the time the study was being worked on, a sixth woman was appointed Cabinet minister, in October 1987.

Issue-specific differences in participation

In which issues is the participation of women high, in which is it low? The two ministries were studied to ascertain differences between them with regard to female participation. Taking all categories of officials into consideration, the Ministry for Foreign Affairs had a higher proportion of women than the Ministry of Defence in all three years, and the difference between the two ministries widened during the period.

Looking at the three categories of officials separately, the differences between the two ministries are great. The Ministry of Defence had a top female official in only one year, 1976/77. The Ministry for Foreign Affairs had top female officials in all three years, and their proportion has increased. Furthermore, in 1976/77 the Minister for Foreign Affairs was a woman.

Among officials responsible for processing issues, the difference between the two ministries is just as great. The participation of women improved at both ministries, but much more rapidly at the Ministry for Foreign Affairs. Only among advisers is the participation of women nearly the same, being only slightly higher at the Ministry for Foreign Affairs.

2. Selected ministerial committees

Bodies examined

Thirty-nine investigations set up by the Ministry of Defence and the Ministry for Foreign Affairs from 1966 to 1987 were studied with regard to female participation. The formal term for such an investigation is ministerial committee, not to be confused with the 16 standing committees of Parliament.

The main task of a ministerial committee is to prepare governmental propositions in different areas. A committee compiles facts, analyses them

and suggests legislation or other action. It therefore holds a strategic
position and is regarded as politically important. A ministerial committee is
always appointed by the Government, which authorizes the Cabinet minister in
question to appoint the members of the committee. 19/ Ministerial committees
are subordinated to the ministries.

There are different forms of ministerial committees. The three most
common are parliamentary appointed committees, one-person committees and civil
servant committees.

There are also different categories of members within a ministerial committee. The most important is the Chairperson (called the Special Investigator
in a one-person committee), who directs the work of the committee. He or she
constitutes, together with the permanent members, the formal committee. The
permanent members, including the Chairperson, have the right of decision and
are responsible for the proposals of the committees. Advisers and experts may
also be included on a committee, but have no right of decision. Advisers work
during the whole session of the committee, while experts are called on only to
help the committee with special information. The day-to-day work, and often
also some of the investigation, is taken care of by one or more secretaries.
20/ A secretary is considered to hold an important position.

Data on representation

Defence-issue bodies

The Ministry of Defence set up 103 ministerial committees from 1966 to
1987; 23 that have great political importance and/or that are of special
interest for this study have been examined (appendix 2B, tables 3a and 4a and
tables for each of the 23 ministerial committees). The members of these 23
ministerial committees have been mapped out by position and sex. Because the
committees generally lasted for long periods of time, their composition
changed. Membership has therefore been counted both at the outset (start) and
towards the end (end).*

The total number of members in the 23 committees including permanent
members and chairpersons or special investigators, advisers, experts and
secretaries (appendix 2B), was 267 at the start, 16 of whom were women (6 per
cent). The highest percentage of women was in the Expert Study on Resistance
Questions as well as in the Committee for a Continued Review of Participation
of Women in the Defence Forces. One fourth of the members of both committees
were women. The greatest number of women (five) was in the 1978 Parliamentary
Committee on Defence Policy. Of the 23 committees, 13 (56 per cent) had no
female members.

At the end, the total number of members was 355, 27 of whom were women
(7.6 per cent). On this occasion the Committee for a Continued Review of
Participation of Women in the Defence Forces had the highest participation of
women, 36 per cent. Together with the 1978 Parliamentary Committee on Defence
Policy, it also had the highest number of women, five. Eight committees, or
35 per cent, had no women.

It seems that women generally enter the work of committees at a later
stage in the life of the committee than do men. Over the working period of

---

*Notice that these ministerial committees were not set up or disbanded at
the same time, although they are counted together in the presentation.

the committees, the participation of women generally increased. In all cases but one, the number of women either stayed the same or increased from thestart to the end. There was also a slight overall increase in the number of women members during the period 1969-1987. The committees formed recently have a higher proportion of female members than the committees formed earlier.

With respect to different categories of members, it can be seen (appendix 2b, table 4a) that at both the start and the end women have their highest representation among permanent members and their lowest among experts, with female participation having ranged between 9 and 13 per cent in the case of permanent members and having been at about 4 per cent in the case of experts. However, about half of all the women in the committees were there as permanent members. Of the permanent members who were women, only one has been a chairperson, in the Committee for a Continued Review of Participation of Women in the Defence Forces.

As was the case among all female members, female permanent members seem to enter the work at a later stage in the life of the committee than male permanent members. Women increased their representation by 100 per cent from start to end among this group, while men increased their participation by only 21 per cent during the same period.

To conclude, it can be seen that women were represented among the permanent members with the right of decision in 5 of the 23 ministerial committees at the start and in 8 at the end.

Foreign affairs/foreign aid-issue bodies

From 1966 to 1987 the Ministry for Foreign Affairs set up 41 investigations, 16 of which have been mapped out. These ministerial committees were also examined with regard to female participation at the start and at the end (see appendix 2B, tables 3b and 4b and tables for each of the committees). Of the 16 committees, 2 became permanent bodies: the Delegation of Disarmament and the Swedish International Humanitarian Law Delegation (appendix 3A, tables C3.1 and D3.1). While they are included here because they were initially treated as ministerial committees, they are also discussed in chapter I.C.1.

At the start, the total number of all members in these 16 committees was 185, of whom 26, or 14 per cent, were women. The highest proportion of women was in a one-person committee, the Committee on the Position of Women, where the special investigator was a woman. The second highest proportion was in the Committee on Swedish Activities Abroad in the Military Equipment Sector as well as in the National Co-ordinating Committee for the United Nations World Population Conference; both had 20 per cent of women members. The highest number of women, four, was in the Delegation of Disarmament together with the Working Group on International Development Assistance Questions. In 4 of the 16 ministerial committees, or 25 per cent, there were no women at the start.

At the end, the total number of female members was 28, or 13 per cent of the 217 members of the 16 committees. The same committees as at the start, except the Committee for the United Nations World Population Conference, had the highest percentage of female members. The highest number of women was, as above, in the Delegation of Disarmament (six). Five of the 16 committees (31 per cent) had no female members at the end.

The participation of women was about the same at both the start and the end. The number of women did increase, but so did the total number of members, leading to a decrease in the proportion of female members on these 16 committees from start to end. If we examine the development of female representation during the period 1967-1987, it can be seen that there was a slightly higher percentage of women in committees appointed during later years.

Focusing on the different categories of members in these 16 committees (see appendix 2b, table 4b), the highest percentage of women, at both the start and the end, was among permanent members, while the lowest was among secretaries. At both the start and the end, approximately 65 per cent of all the women in these 16 committees held positions as permanent members, both at the start and the end, with the right of decision. Six of the women at the start were either chairpersons or special investigators. At the end, five women held these positions.

In summary, women participated as permanent members in 9 of the 16 ministerial committees (56 per cent) at both the start and the end.

Comparison with ministerial committees of all the ministries (1986)

The total number of ministerial committees at work, that is, subordinated to all ministries, was 218 during 1985/86. About 3,500 persons were members of these committees, 17 per cent of them women. The lowest proportion of women was among chairpersons, the highest among secretaries (table 9). 21/

Table 9. All ministerial committees by position and sex, 1986

Position	Number of		
	Women	Men	Women, %
Chairperson a/	18	219	8
Permanent member	153	617	20
Adviser or expert	321	1 747	16
Secretary b/	98	316	24
Total	590	2 899	17

Source: Statistics Sweden (SCB), Kvinno- och Mansvär(l)den: Fakta om jämställdheten i Sverige 1986 (Stockholm, Norstedts Tryckeri, 1986), p. 172.

a/ Including special investigator.

b/ Both permanent and deputy secretaries.

Ninety per cent of the ministerial committees were led by men. The differences between the ministerial committees of the different ministries are great. The highest proportion of female chairpersons (29 per cent) prevailed in ministerial committees subordinated to the Ministry of Labour, while the Ministry of Health and Social Affairs had the highest number of female chairpersons (six). Among the 770 permanent members of all 218 ministerial committees, not including chairpersons, 20 per cent were women. Only the Ministry of Health and Social Affairs had nearly an equal number of men and women on its committees, 45 per cent women and 55 per cent men. 22/

Discussion

Overall trend

From 1966 to 1987, the percentage of female members (all categories) increased. However, only one committee achieved a representation of 40 per cent women and over half of the committees had no female participation at all (appendix 2B, tables 3a and 3b).

Participation in important posts

Which positions are normally held, or not held, by women within these 39 ministerial committees? Has the picture changed? If all the members of the 39 ministerial committees are counted, the highest participation of women is seen to be among the permanent members, where they constitute a one-seventh part. This can be compared with the participation of women in committees set up by all the ministries in 1986, in which women constituted a one-sixth part.* However, over 50 per cent of all the women were permanent members having the right of decision.

In the committees examined in this study there was one female chairperson among the committees appointed by the Ministry of Defence and six (five at the end) among the committees appointed by the Ministry for Foreign Affairs, which amounts to 4 per cent and 37 per cent (31 per cent), respectively. The difference is striking, both between these two ministries and compared to the committees from all ministries (8 per cent). The Ministry for Foreign Affairs generally has a higher percentage of female chairpersons in the committees studied here than in other committees subordinated to other ministries (table 9).

In the 39 committees, the lowest proportion of women, less than 6 per cent, was among the secretaries. That proportion should be compared with the proportion in table 9, which is 24 per cent. More research has to be carried out to learn why these differences occur. It may be that secretaries are recruited mainly from the ministries and thus reflect the share of women there.

It is also interesting to examine who appointed these committees, specifically, if they were men or women and if women appointed more women. As was already noted, the members of a ministerial committee are appointed by the Cabinet minister in question. From October 1976 to October 1978, the Ministry for Foreign Affairs was directed by a woman. During this period two of the 16 committees of the Ministry for Foreign Affairs were appointed. One was a one-person committee, a man. The second was a parliamentary-appointed committee with 3 female permanent members out of a total of 13. The Chairperson was a man.

These examples are too few to allow drawing general conclusions. To establish if female ministers appoint more women to ministerial committees than male ministers, it would be necessary to examine all the ministries and the ministerial committees subordinated to them and compare periods when there were female ministers with periods when there were male ministers.

---

*Calculated from data in table 9. Including both chairpersons and permanent members, as these two are in the same category in the statistical data in appendix 2B, the calculation is: (18 + 153)/[(18 + 153) + (219 + 617)] = 0.17, or 17 per cent.

Bodies ranked by political importance

Is the participation of women great or small in politically important decision-making bodies? The differences in political importance between these ministerial committees are hard to quantify. However, the parliamentary committees on defence policy may justifiably be regarded as more important than the other committees. The committees on defence policy are appointed every fifth year and are responsible for formulating plans for Swedish national defence for the coming five years. During 1966-1987, five such committees were set up (appendix 2B, tables B2.2.1, B2.2.9, B2.2.16, B2.2.22 and B2.2.23); they will be examined here with regard to female representation.

Of all 119 (144) members of these five committees, 8 were women.* Of these women, five and six, respectively, were permanent members.** Not one woman was a chairperson. Moreover, few were advisers or experts, and none was a secretary. Since only permanent members have the right of decision, it can be said that few women had influence in the parliamentary committees on defence policy (see appendix 2B, tables 3a and 3b).***

Having looked for differences with regard to the average number of women in the three types of ministerial committee, that is, parliamentary appointed committees, one-person committees and civil servant committees, it can be concluded that there are no significant differences from one type of committee to the other. What emerged, however, was the difference between the average number of women and the average number of men who are permanent members: there were in general more men than women in the 39 ministerial committees. When the average number of men and women permanent members at the start and the end is calculated, the result is 0.6 women and 3.8 men on the average at the start. The corresponding figures at the end are 0.8 women and 4.7 men (see appendix 2B, tables 4a and 4b).****

Issue-specific differences in participation

In which issues is the representation of women high, in which is it low? The ministerial committees in which the participation of women has been highest are those that deal with women's issues. In the Committee for a Continued Review of Participation of Women in the Defence Forces and the Committee on the Positions of Women, female members dominated. These 2 committees had the highest participation of women (67 per cent and 100 per cent) of all 39 committees.

---

*The total number of members was 119 at the start and 144 at the end, which amounts to female participation of 6.7 per cent and 5.6 per cent, respectively.

**That is, 12.5 per cent at the start and 13.3 per cent at the end.

***The total number of members in all 39 ministerial committees was 452 at the start and 527 at the end. In the defence committees, only five and six women, respectively, were permanent members, with the right of decision (5/452 = 1.1 per cent, 6/572 = 1 per cent). In the ministerial committees set up by the Ministry of Defence, there were altogether 267 and 355 members, respectively (5/267 = 1.9 per cent, 6/355 = 1.7 per cent).

****Calculated as follows: (7 + 17)/39 = 0.6 women on average at the start and (14 + 18)/39 = 0.82 women at the end; (74 + 73)/39 = 3.77 men on the average at the start and (96 + 89)/39 = 4.74 men at the end.

There were also some differences between committees set up by the
Ministry of Defence and those set up by the Ministry for Foreign Affairs.
First, in committees subordinated to the Ministry of Defence, women generally
seemed to enter the work of a committee at a later stage in its life than
men. This was not true in committees subordinated to the Ministry for Foreign
Affairs.

Secondly, there were on average more female participants in committees
set up by the Ministry for Foreign Affairs. In each of these committees there
were, on average, 1.7 women if all the categories of members were included.
In committees set up by the Ministry of Defence only 0.9 women participated on
average (appendix 2B, tables 3a and 3b).* If only permanent members are taken
into account, the difference becomes even greater.

Thirdly, even if the number of women is higher on average in foreign
affairs committees, the percentage of women is generally not higher. However,
the spread of women, that is, the number of committees in which they participated, is more balanced for these committees than for committees subordinated
to the Ministry of Defence. This difference did, however, become less pronounced during the period studied. At the start, there were no women in
56 per cent of the committees set up by the Ministry of Defence. At the end,
35 per cent of these committees had no female participation. The corresponding
figures for the Ministry for Foreign Affairs are 25 per cent and 33 per cent.

Fourthly, there was a higher percentage of female chairpersons and/or
special investigators among committees set up by the Ministry for Foreign
Affairs than among those set up by the Ministry of Defence.

C. Women in decision-making bodies within Swedish governmental authorities

In this section, two classes of bodies will be analysed with respect to
the participation of women: the central governmental authorities (chapter I.C.1)
and the diplomatic service and Swedish delegations abroad (chapter I.C.2).
The diplomatic service and Swedish delegations abroad are presented separately
because they are not formally regarded as decision-making bodies. They are,
however, important in so far as they can be regarded as an extension of the
Ministry for Foreign Affairs. Ambassadors and members of delegations
implement Swedish foreign policy.

1. Central governmental authorities

Bodies examined

Central governmental authorities consist of civil service departments
(ämbetsverk) and other central governmental authorities. Civil service departments are usually defined as those authorities that fulfil four criteria:
(a) the authority is under the direct jurisdiction of the Government, that
is, of the Government as a whole, not just the Cabinet minister responsible
for the ministry; (b) its appropriations come through the ministry it is

---

*The number of ministerial committees set up by the Ministry for Foreign
Affairs was 16. The corresponding figure for the Ministry of Defence was 23.
If women are counted both at the start and at the end, the average number of
women in each of the 16 committees set up by the Ministry for Foreign Affairs
becomes (26 + 28)/(16 + 16) = 1.69. The corresponding figure for each
committee set up by the Ministry Defence becomes (16 + 27)/(23 + 23) = 0.93.

administratively subordinated to (<u>avlämnar petita</u>); (c) its area of responsibility is nation-wide; and (d) it is organized into departments and/or offices (<u>avdelningar/byraer</u>). Altogether there are about 80 civil service departments. The other central governmental authorities, approximately 100, do not fulfil all these criteria; usually they are small boards of laymen or experts. <u>23</u>/

A civil service department, especially one that has important political or economic responsibility, is usually controlled by a board of laymen (<u>lekmannastyrelse</u>) that has the director-general of the department as its chairperson. The laymen, who have no function in a civil service department other than as a member of its board, can be government officials, politicians, often members of the Riksdag, or representatives of public interest organizations. It is now common for officials employed at an authority to have their own representatives on the board (<u>personalföreträdare</u>). They would, however, be subject to special conditions and have limited rights of decision. In a civil service department that is not governed by a board of laymen, the director-general alone is in charge. <u>24</u>/

This inquiry focuses on civil service departments and other central governmental authorities subordinated to the Ministry of Defence and the Ministry for Foreign Affairs. The following authorities dealing with defence issues and subordinated to the Ministry of Defence have been examined: the Armed Forces of the National Defence;* the Defence Materiel Administration; the National Board of Civil Defence, Rescue and Fire Services; the National Board of Psychological Defence; the National Board of Economic Defence; and the Office of the Director, Regional Civilian Defence Area.

The only authority dealing exclusively with disarmament issues, the Delegation of Disarmament (subordinated to the Ministry for Foreign Affairs), has been transformed from a ministerial committee into a permanent authority (see chapter I.B.2). It is basically a consultative authority that holds four or five meetings a year and is organized like a ministerial committee, with permanent members, experts and a secretariat. The Chairperson is also the Ambassador of Disarmament and head of the Swedish Disarmament Commission at the Ministry for Foreign Affairs (see chapter I.B.1). A senior administrative officer employed at the Disarmament Commission is also the secretary of the authority. The Swedish Delegation to the Conference on Disarmament at Geneva is subordinated to the Ambassador of Disarmament (see chapter I.C.2).**

Of the decision-making bodies responsible for issues concerning foreign affairs and foreign aid and which are subordinate to the Foreign Ministry, the following have been examined: the Swedish International Humanitarian Law Delegation, the Swedish International Development Authority (SIDA), the Swedish Board for Education in International Development, the Consultative Committee on Humanitarian Assistance and the Advisory Council on Development-Co-operation Issues. The Swedish International Humanitarian Law Committee had been a ministerial committee but is now a permanent authority.

---

*The Armed Forces of the National Defence: The Supreme Commander of the Armed Forces (including staff) and the Defence Staff; the Head of the Army (including staff) and the Army Staff; the Head of the Navy (including staff) and the Naval Staff; the Head of the Air Forces and the Air Staff; the Head of the National Home Guard and the National Home Guard Staff.

**Information on this organization has been received from the Ministry for Foreign Affairs and the Ambassador of Disarmament.

It is still organized like a committee, with permanent members, experts, advisers and a secretariat. SIDA is a civil service department, while the three other bodies are small boards made up of laymen or experts.

The political importance of these authorities is hard to estimate because they have different tasks and areas of responsibility. SIDA is regarded as politically important because it has primary responsibility for implementing the Swedish development co-operation aid programme.

Since these bodies are of different types they have different categories of employees. Employees at the highest levels, such as members of boards and top officials, and when possible, that is, when such employees exist, employees at the level of officials responsible for processing an issue or matter have been included in this survey. Layman/expert boards sometimes have staffs, and wherever possible these are included in the statistical figures. In the two delegations, permanent members, experts, advisers and secretaries have been included (see the tables in appendix 3A).

Data on representation

Defence-issue bodies

There are few women in the 10 authorities examined here that deal with defence issues. If all included employees in the authorities are taken into consideration, the proportion of women was 4 per cent in 1986/87 and about 1 per cent in the other two years (see appendix 3A, table 1 and tables B3.1-B3.10).

In the Armed Forces of the National Defence, there were no women, except in 1986/87, when two women (1 per cent) were heads of departments. In the Defence Materiel Administration, which was established in 1968, there were no women in 1976/77 and 9 out of 180 in 1986/87 (5 per cent). Two of them were head officials, the rest were officials responsible for processing issues. There were no women on the board of this authority. At the Office of the Director, Regional Civilian Defence Areas, there have not been any women.

The three boards composed of laymen or experts generally had greater female participation than the authorities discussed above. On the National Board of Civil Defence, Rescue and Fire Services, female participation was 5-6 per cent in all three years, although the number of women was only two at the most. On the National Board of Economic Defence, female participation increased in later years, from 0 per cent in 1976/77 to 11 per cent in 1986/87 (five women). On the National Board of Psychological Defence, female participation increased from 7 per cent in 1966/67 (one woman) to 12 per cent in 1976/77 (two women) but then decreased to 0 per cent in 1986/87. Between 1976/77 and 1986/87 the total number of persons in this authority also decreased.

Disarmament-issue body

The Delegation of Disarmament (appendix 3A, tables 2 and C3.1), the only authority dealing exclusively with disarmament issues, is surveyed with respect to the participation of women both at the start, when it had been established as a ministerial committee (see explanation in chapter I.B.2 and first page of appendix 2B) and at the end (October 1987). The participation of women was 17 per cent at the start and 19 per cent at the end, counting all members. Among permanent members, who have the right of decision, the proportion of female participants was higher, 18 per cent and 30 per cent, respectively. The Chairperson was a woman, although not the same woman, at both the start and the end (see also chapter I.B.2).

Foreign affairs/foreign aid-issue bodies

When authorities dealing with foreign affairs and foreign aid are examined, it can be seen that the participation of women has been 22 per cent or less during the period when all authorities are counted together (appendix 3A, table 3). The participation of women was different in these authorities, with regard to both the development of, as well as the percentage of, female participation.

In SIDA, a civil service department, female participation increased steadily, counting all included employees, from 7 per cent to 27 per cent. In the Swedish International Humanitarian Law Delegation, the situation was different: of all included members, only one was a woman, in 1976/77.

For the three layman/expert boards included here, the picture was ambiguous. In the Consultative Committee on Humanitarian Assistance, the only board of this type that existed in 1966/67, female participation decreased from 14 per cent to 10 per cent, although the number of women increased from one to two. In the other two boards, development has been the other way round: from no women included in 1976/77, participation grew to 44 per cent and 31 per cent, respectively, in 1986/87 (four women in each). The figures for these three authorities include only members of their boards.

Comparison with boards of 82 central governmental authorities (1986)

To enable a comparison to be made between female representation in authorities dealing only with defence, disarmament, foreign affairs and foreign aid and female representation in authorities dealing with other issues, the heads and boards of 82 authorities were enumerated. As is seen in table 10, 5 of the 82 authorities were headed by women, and 9 had female chairpersons.*
In the lowest category the deputy representatives of the officials (personalföreträdare, suppleanter), female participation the highest. 25/

Table 10. Heads and boards of central governmental authorities
by position and sex, 1 April 1986

Position	Women		Men		Both sexes	
	Number	%	Number	%	Number	%
Director-General	5	6	77	94	82	100
Deputy Director-General	6	9	65	91	71	100
Chairperson on the board	9	11	74	89	83	100
Deputy Chairperson	4	7	50	93	54	100
Permanent members not including chairpersons, deputy chairpersons or representatives of the officials	117	19	515	81	632	100

continued

*Usually the head of the authority and the chairperson are the same person.

Table 10 (<u>continued</u>)

Position	Women		Men		Both sexes	
	Number	%	Number	%	Number	%
Deputy members not including represen- tatives of the officials	39	23	128	77	167	100
Representatives of the officials, permanent	35	25	106	75	141	100
Representatives of the officials, deputy	38	34	74	66	112	100

<u>Source</u>: <u>Ska även morgondagens samhälle formas enbart au män</u>? (Ministry of Labour, Stockholm, DSA 1986:4), pp. 20 and 107.

Discussion

Overall trend

If all categories of employees included here are taken into consideration, the overall trend in the 16 central governmental authorities is that female participation has increased, although only slightly. The development of female participation differs, however, from one authority to the next (table 11). The only authority that had over 40 per cent female participation was the Swedish Board for Education in International Development, in 1986/87.

Table 11. Female representation in each of the 16 central governmental authorities
(Percentage)

Government authority	1966/67	1976/77	1986/87
Supreme Commander/Defence Staff	0	0	2
Head of Army/Army Staff	0	0	3
Head of Navy/Naval Staff	0	0	0
Head of Air Force/Air Staff	0	0	0
Head of National Home Guard (NHG)/NHG Staff	0	0	0
Defence Materiel Administration	-	0	5
National Board of Civil Defence, Rescue and Fire Services	5	6	5
National Board of Psychological Defence	7	12	0
National Board of Economic Defence	0	0	11
Office of Director, Regional Civilian Defence Area	0	0	0
Delegation of Disarmament		17 a/	19 a/

continued

Table 11 (continued)

Government authority	1966/67	1976/77	1986/87
Swedish International Humanitarian			
Law Delegation		6 a/	0 a/
Swedish International Development Authority	7	16	27
Swedish Board for Education in			
International Development	–	0	44
Consultative Committee on Humanitarian			
Assistance	14	10	10
Advisory Council on Development			
Co-operation Issues	–	0	29

Source: Appendix 3A, tables B3.1-3.10, C3.1 and D3.1-3.5.

a/ Figures show "start" and "end" rather than the three years referred to elsewhere in this report; see appendix 3A, tables C3.1 and D3.1 and explanation in chapter I.B.2 as well as appendix 2B, p. 1.

Participation in important posts

Which positions are normally held by women in these central governmental authorities? Has the picture changed over time? Eight of the 16 authorities have a board as the highest level of decision-making.* Female participation in these boards is very different. The highest proportion of women was on the board of SIDA in 1976/77 (27 per cent), the lowest on the boards of the Defence Materiel Administration and the National Board of Economic Defence, neither of which had women in any of the three years.

Two of the defence-issue bodies have had female members on their boards, while two have not.** It seems that if there have been women on the board for a longer period, the authority tries to continue to include one or two women. When the total number of members on the board decreases, the number of women falls. This was the case at both the National Board of Civil Defence and the National Board of Psychological Defence. At the former, the total number of members on the board decreased from 10 to 9 between 1976/77 and 1986/87. At the same time, the number of women decreased from 2 to 1 (from 20 per cent to 11 per cent). At the National Board of Psychological Defence, there were 16 persons on the board in 1976/77, 2 of whom were women (12 per cent). In 1986/87 there were 9 members on the board and no women. It would be interesting to learn if this is a general pattern for board representation.

---

*All but the Armed Forces of the National Defence; the Office of the Director, Regional Civilian Defence Area; and the two delegations.

**The Defence Materiel Administration and the National Board of Economic Defence did not have women on their boards in 1966/67, 1976/77 or 1986/87. The National Board of Civil Defence, Rescue and Fire Services and the National Board of Psychological Defence had women on their boards in all three years (see appendix 3A, tables B3.6-B3.9).

All four bodies dealing with foreign affairs and foreign aid had female members on their boards, either in all three years or in 1986/87.* Also, here a custom seems to have developed: if women had been on the board for a longer period, there were also female members in 1986/87. However, neither on the board of SIDA nor in the Consultative Committee on Humanitarian Affairs, both of which existed during the whole period, has the number of women increased proportionally to the total number of members. Thus, female participation on the boards has declined.**

The Swedish Board for Education in International Development and the Advisory Council on Development Co-operation Issues had women participants only in 1986/87, but then at a fairly high rate: 44 per cent and 31 per cent, respectively.

Data for two of the authorities, the Defence Materiel Administration and SIDA, also includes top officials and officials responsible for processing issues. Are there differences in female participation from one category of employee to another in these authorities?

In the Defence Materiel Administration, there were only 9 women out of 180 in 1986/87 and no women in 1976/77. Of these women, none were on the board, two were heads of divisions and the remaining seven were officials responsible for processing issues.

In SIDA, total female participation increased from 1966/67 to 1986/87, from 7 per cent to 27 per cent. In which categories of employee did the increases come? It can be seen (appendix 3A, table D3.2) that in 1966/67 and 1976/77 the highest female participation was on the board, followed by top officials; the lowest female participation was among officials responsible for processing issues. By 1986/87 this picture had changed: the highest participation of women was now among the officials responsible for processing issues, followed by top officials and finally by the board. This would mean that as the total number of female employees increased, they were employed in lower echelons. This, too, would seem to be a fruitful field for future inquiry.

Data for the Armed Forces of the National Defence and the Office of the Director, Regional Civilian Defence Area, includes top officials and staff. As there are so few women in these bodies, it is hard to discern any trend or pattern. The only two women, in 1986/87, were both heads of departments.

---

*There have been women on the boards of SIDA and the Consultative Committee on Humanitarian Affairs in all three years. On the boards of the Swedish Board for Education in International Development and the Advisory Council on Development Co-operation Issues, neither of which existed in 1966/67, there were women in 1986/87 (see appendix 3A, tables D3.2-D3.5).

**In SIDA the total number of members on the board was 9 in 1966/67, 11 in 1976/77 and 14 in 1986/87, while the number of women was one, three and three, respectively. This amounts to female participation of 11.1 per cent, 27.3 per cent and 21.4 per cent, respectively. For the Consultative Committee on Humanitarian Affairs, the corresponding figures are 7, 10 and 21 (all members) and 1, 1 and 2 (women) = 14.3, 10.0 and 9.5 per cent (see appendix 3A, tables D3.2 and D3.4).

For two of the authorities, the Delegation of Disarmament and the Swedish International Humanitarian Law Delegation, the statistics include four categories of members: permanent members, experts, special advisers and secretaries. In both delegations, the highest participation of women was among the permanent members and the lowest among the secretaries, both at the start and at the end. It is, however, necessary to point out that in the Swedish International Humanitarian Law Delegation, only one woman participated, as one of two permanent members at the start (see chapter I.B.2).

Issue-specific differences in participation

Among Government authorities, the highest participation of women is in the body dealing with disarmament issues, followed by the bodies dealing with foreign affairs and foreign aid. The lowest participation of women is in the bodies dealing with defence issues. The low participation of women in authorities dealing with defence issues can be partly explained by the fact that employees in authorities dealing with defence issues are to a great extent recruited from military professionals. Since women were not allowed to become officers in the military before 1983 they have in effect been excluded from that particular recruitment base.

2. The diplomatic service and delegations

Bodies examined

This section looks first at Swedish embassies, the Permanent Mission of Sweden to the United Nations, New York, and Sweden's Permanent Mission to the International Organizations at Geneva, including the Swedish Delegation to the Conference on Disarmament at Geneva. For these bodies, the data cover 1966/67, 1976/77 and 1986/87. The persons surveyed are the ambassadors and, in the case of delegations, the permanent delegates (appendix 3B, tables D3.6.1, D3.7.1A-1C).

It looks next at the Swedish delegations to the European Conference on Security and Co-operation 1975 to 1987, to the First Committee of the United Nations General Assembly, 1978 to 1986,* to the first two special sessions of the General Assembly devoted to Disarmament, one in 1978 and one in 1982, and to the World Conference on Disarmament and Development in 1987 (appendix 3B, tables D3.7.2-D3.7.5).

These authorities are not regarded as formal decision-making bodies since they are all subordinated to the Ministry for Foreign Affairs. Their work, however, serves an important purpose in peace and disarmament policy.

The Swedish Delegation to the Conference on Disarmament at Geneva has a top official based at Geneva and responsible for the work there. The Ambassador of Disarmament, based at Stockholm, is the head of the delegation.**

---

*The First Committee has been responsible for disarmament issues since 1978, which is the reason for this particular set of years.

**Information received from the Ambassador of Disarmament.

Data on representation

Ambassadors

There were few female ambassadors stationed abroad. In 1966/67, there was one and in 1986/87 there were two. The total number of ambassadors abroad increased from 56 to 63 and 78 in the respective years (appendix 3B, table D3.6.1).

Members of delegations

There were almost no women in the permanent delegations of Sweden.* In delegations to international conferences, the proportion of women varied. In the Swedish delegations to the European Conference on Security and Co-operation (1973-1987), the participation of women varied between 0 per cent and 25 per cent (permanent delegates). The largest number of women, 4 out of 19, or 21 per cent, was at Stockholm in 1986, while the largest percentage of women was at Vienna in 1987 (25 per cent, one out of four).** At two of the five conferences, there were no women (appendix 3B, table D3.7.2).

In all Swedish delegations to the United Nations General Assembly, First Committee, 1978 to 1986, women were included. Female participation varied between 15 per cent (1982) and 37 per cent (1978/79), and the largest number of women was seven (in 1978/79, 1983 and 1985), while the lowest was three (1982). The figures include permanent members (ombud) and substitutes for permanent members (ersättare för ombud) (appendix 3B, table D3.7.3).

There were three women in each of the Swedish delegations to the first two special sessions of the General Assembly devoted to Disarmament (1978 and 1982) and the Swedish delegation to the World Conference on Disarmament and Development (1987). The proportion varied between 27 per cent (1978) and 38 per cent (1987). These figures include both permanent members and substitutes (appendix 3B, tables D3.7.4 and D3.7.5).

Some of the delegations to international conferences also included advisers or experts. The number of women in these two categories was low, the highest number being four, although generally at least one woman was included. At one conference, however, there were no women. The highest proportion of female advisers/experts was 25 per cent, one out of four, but in all other cases, the proportion varied between 3 and 12 per cent (see footnotes to tables D3.7.2-D3.7.5 in appendix 3B).

Comparison with all employees of embassies

According to information received from the Ministry for Foreign Affairs, the total number of persons employed at Swedish embassies abroad in 1987 was 627, of whom 292, or 47 per cent, were women. Of these women, 210 had administrative posts, that is, 72 per cent of all the women stationed abroad at embassies. Of the remaining 82 women, or 13 per cent of all persons

---

*In 1986/87 there were, altogether, nine permanent delegations of Sweden, only two of which have been more closely examined. In general, however, there were no women, or very few, in the nine delegations (see appendix 3B, tables D3.7.1A-1C).

**At the preparatory meeting in Belgrade, there were two delegates, one man and one woman.

employed abroad, four were at the highest level; this amounted to less than 1 per cent of all persons stationed abroad and slightly more than 1 per cent of all the women.

According to the same source, of the 335 men employed at embassies abroad, 15 had administrative posts, that is, 4 per cent of all men. Of the remaining 320 men, or 51 per cent of all personnel stationed abroad, 99 were at the top level, that is, 16 per cent of all personnel stationed abroad and 30 per cent of all the men. Thus, women dominated at the lower echelons, while men dominated at the higher.

Discussion

What is the extent of female participation among ambassadors and among delegates of the 20 delegations? Among ambassadors and among permanent delegations, female representation is low. Among Swedish delegations to international conferences, it is higher.

To what can this difference be ascribed? In the first category, ambassadors, where there were very few women, recruitment is from among officials employed at the Ministry for Foreign Affairs. In the second category, delegations to international conferences, in which more women are included, most of the delegates are members of the Riksdag.

This difference can be seen even more clearly by focusing on delegations to international conferences. In Swedish delegations to the European Conference on Security and Co-operation, apart from the conference that took place at Stockholm, all the delegates were officials; there were either no female delegates or only one. Of the delegation to the conference at Stockholm, 9 were officials and 6 were members of the Riksdag, a total of 15. Of these, three were women, all of them members of the Riksdag.*

In the remaining delegations to international conferences, the majority of the delegates were members of the Riksdag. All the women except one were members of the Riksdag.** The woman who was not a member was Secretary of State,*** having been a delegate to the two special sessions of the General Assembly devoted to Disarmament. This suggests that when members of the Riksdag are appointed as delegates, more women are included.

Officials can be classified as to their importance from the standpoint of decision-making by their titles. Ambassadors are in an important position; as we have seen, there were few women among them. In the delegations, there were two women with titles, one a Senior Administrative Officer, a rather low position, and the other a Counsellor, a high position.****

_____

*One woman was both a member of the Riksdag and the Ambassador of Disarmament, as well as the Chairperson of the Delegation of Disarmament.

**See preceding footnote.

***This person had previously been Chairperson of the Delegation of Disarmament.

****These two persons were delegates to the conferences at Belgrade and Vienna, respectively. In the second, third and fourth session of the conference at Madrid, there was one woman delegate who was Administrative Officer, which is a lower rank than Senior Administrative Officer. See appendix 3B, table D3.7.2.

Delegations to international conferences have both permanent members and substitutes. However, in all cases but four the data sources do not show these two categories separately. Of these four, two have a higher percentage of women among the substitutes than among the permanent members. Female participation was higher among substitutes than among permanent members in 1978. In 1982 and 1987 the reverse was true.

D. Summary

This summary will point out the differences as well as the similarities between the decision-making bodies examined in chapter I. In all, 72 different decision-making bodies within the areas of defence, disarmament, foreign affairs and foreign aid have been examined. Twenty-six of these bodies are permanent authorities within either the Riksdag, the Government and the Government Office, or the central governmental authorities. They were studied at three points in time: 1966/67, 1976/77 and 1986/87. Thirty-nine of the bodies were ministerial committees set up by the Ministry of Defence or the Ministry for Foreign Affairs from 1966 to 1986. Each committee was examined on two occasions: when it was set up ("start") and towards the end ("end").

Twenty Swedish delegations, permanent ones as well as those appointed to international conferences, were also studied. Permanent delegations abroad were analysed at three points in time, 1966/67, 1976/77 and 1986/87, while delegations to international conferences from 1973 to 1987 were studied on one occasion each (see summary table on page 1 of the annex for an overview).

Female participation in the 72 decision-making bodies was thus registered on a total of 182 occasions. For comparison purposes, the participation of women in bodies dealing with other issues has also been included.

The participation of women in these bodies generally increased during the period 1966/67 to 1986/87. The increase has varied, however, from one decision-making body to another. On average, if all the decisionmaking bodies studied on the three occasions are taken into consideration and all the included persons are counted, the participation of women rose from approximately 6 per cent in 1966/67 to 19 per cent in 1986/87.

The body in which female participation increased the most since 1966/67 is the Office of the Prime Minister. In 1986/87 the highest percentage of women could be found in the Swedish Delegation to the Nordic Council, the Office of the Prime Minister and the Swedish Board for Education in International Development, all of which had 40 per cent or more of women, all included persons counted.

Although the participation of women increased in general, it seems that the increase at higher levels of decision-making was not as great as the general increase. In some cases, there was either a declining or an unchanged proportion of female members of boards and of top officials, accompanied by an increasing proportion of female officials responsible for processing issues.* Two different pictures emerge: either the percentage of female members of

_____

*For example, see SIDA, the Consultative Committee on Humanitarian Affairs, the Ministry of Defence and the Ministry for Foreign Affairs.

boards and top officials declined while the percentage of female officials
increased, or female participation increased in both categories, but much more
in the latter.

A related development is that in decision-making bodies where the members
were either permanent or deputy members, the percentage of women among
permanent members declined while among deputy members it increased. This
development was most marked between 1976/77 and 1986/87.

There were, in general, few female chairpersons and top officials in
these decision-making bodies. When all included chairpersons and the highest
top official in all the units were counted, they numbered 165; 11 of them were
women, that is approximately 7 per cent, with all decision-making bodies and
all studied occasions included. However, one group of decision-making bodies
diverged from the overall pattern: of the 11 women, 6 were chairpersons in
ministerial committees set up by the Ministry for Foreign Affairs. Altogether,
16 committees subordinated to this Ministry were studied. Thus, 37 per cent
of all the chairpersons in this type of decision-making body were women, a
much higher proportion than in decision-making bodies overall.*

The impression remains that women are more often found in positions that
are regarded as less important. The majority of the women appointed as Cabinet
ministers were consultative ministers rather than ministers responsible for a
ministry.

However, the situation in ministerial committees differed in this regard.
Indeed, when the members of the ministerial committees were categorized by
type, that is, as permanent member, adviser, expert or secretary, the greatest
participation of women was found to be among the permanent members. Thus,
even if it is generally true that women get less important positions, this is
not always the case.

Moreover, the tendency for women to be found in less important positions
became more pronounced in the latter part of the period 1966/67-1986/87. For
example, in 1986/87 the situation in bodies having both permanent and deputy
members was that women were more often deputy rather than permanent members.
If this is the general trend, it might explain the difference observed in
female participation among chairpersons in the ministerial committees. In all
ministerial committees for 1986 there was an 8 per cent incidence of female
chairpersons, while in those examined over a longer period of time, for
example, all committees appointed by the Ministry for Foreign Affairs, the
incidence of female chairpersons was much higher.**

Furthermore, politically important bodies have generally had fewer women
than politically less important bodies. This is true for all issues examined
and at all levels of decision-making bodies, that is, in bodies within the
Riksdag and in the Government and the Government Office and in central
governmental authorities.

---

*Six at the start and five at the end, or 37 per cent and 31 per cent,
respectively, of all 16 chairpersons.

**Even if the ministerial committees subordinated to the Ministry of
Defence, in which the number of female chairpersons is few, are counted
together with the committees subordinated to the Ministry for Foreign Affairs,
the total number of and percentage of female chairpersons is higher than in
the other decision-making bodies.

Concentrating on the variation in the participation of women from issue to issue, it can be seen that there are fewer women involved in bodies dealing with defence issues than in bodies dealing with disarmament and foreign affairs or foreign aid. This is a clear pattern, the explanation for which may be that, until recently, women had been excluded from military careers. Not permitted to become a member of the armed forces, a woman could not therefore join the Armed Forces of the National Defence, except as an administrative official. Furthermore, most of the people employed at the Ministry of Defence are former or present members of the armed forces, implying that, although such may not have been formal policy, women have also been excluded from the ministry that deals with defence issues. Issue-specific differences in female representation also seem to have become more pronounced during the period: although female participation increased in both kinds of bodies, it increased more rapidly in bodies that deal with foreign affairs issues.

Another observation is that if parliamentarians were included in the body, there was usually a higher proportion of women than if only officials were included. This is most clearly exemplified by the Swedish delegations.

II. WOMEN AND DECISION-MAKING: INSIGHTS FROM INTERVIEWS

This chapter is based on the data in chapter I as well as on interviews with eight women and four men holding decision-making posts in the areas of defence, disarmament, foreign affairs or foreign aid. Their replies form the basis for the discussion here. As agreed beforehand, the individuals are not quoted nor are opinions attributed to particular persons.

The interviewed persons were selected primarily because of their positions in the decision-making bodies that were being examined.* The second criterion for selection, applied to the eight women, was that each must have been a member of at least three of the decision-making bodies studied here. The final criterion was that each had to have been a member of the Riksdag in 1986/87. The four men, who were members of the Riksdag as well as members of some of the other bodies studied, were not selected in the same systematic way. They were interviewed to learn if they had the same opinions as the eight women, not to learn if they had encountered obstacles.

Because this chapter is based on interviews with a relatively small number of persons, the conclusions it draws must be seen as hypotheses that need careful testing.

A. Means for achieving positions of power

Of the eight women interviewed, six became members of the Riksdag during the 1970s and two during the latter part of the 1960s. Within the Riksdag and its authorities they all held posts either as permanent or deputy members of the Standing Committee on Foreign Affairs or the Standing Committee on Defence. Four had been delegates in the Swedish Delegation to the Nordic Council and one had been on the Executive Committee of the Interparliamentary Group. Three had been members of the Advisory Council on Foreign Affairs, two had been members of the War Delegation and three had been permanent members of the Delegation of Disarmament. All but three had been delegates to the United Nations General Assembly.

Outside the Riksdag they had held other important posts, in their parties as well as in other bodies, for example, as Head of the Ministry for Foreign Affairs, as Ambassador of Disarmament, as members of the board of SIDA or as permanent members of the parliamentary committees on defence policy (ministerial committees). The men had also held, and still hold, important posts in the decision-making bodies discussed here, for example, as permanent members of the Standing Committee on Foreign Affairs or as chairpersons and deputy chairpersons in this Committee, in the Standing Committee on Defence or in the Executive Committee of the Interparliamentary Group.

Within their parties, the areas of responsibility of these men and women differed. They were often interested in more than one issue. Three had defence and security policy as their main area of competence, and three had the broad area of foreign affairs. Disarmament and foreign aid were the main competence of six persons.

---

*Initially, nine women and five men had been selected, but two were not able to participate.

When examining the career paths of these men and women within the Riksdag, that is, their positions in the standing committees after having entered the Riksdag, it is hard to discern a pattern. All except one of the men started as deputy members of committees where their responsibilities included neither foreign affairs nor defence,* and they had varying careers after that.

It may be that women often have a longer way to travel than men before reaching a high position, and not only in the standing committees. If this is true, a woman would, for example, tend to start as a deputy member of a less important committee; be appointed, in turn, a permanent member of this committee, a deputy member of a more important committee, a permanent member of the more important committee; and, finally, perhaps, become chairperson or deputy chairperson. According to this theory, a man would start at the same low level but would then get an important position in an important body more quickly than a woman.

However, a clear pattern cannot be inferred from the experience of these twelve persons only. The time it takes to reach high positions, as well as the political importance of the different committees, would have to be examined much more carefully before firm conclusions could be drawn. It would also be important to learn if men's and women's careers proceed differently in different fields. All these matters could be subjects for further study.

When a person becomes a member of the Riksdag, he or she is given the opportunity to specify which committees he or she would like to join. The parties may take these wishes into consideration when they nominate their members to committees. However, there are many other considerations, for example, the party's strength, that is, how many seats it gets in each committee; the qualifications of the person; the relative seniority of other aspirants to the post,** and so on.

The question of individual preference may partly explain how these men and women came to be associated with one or another of the issues studied in this report. Of the eight women, six said they had had either a great deal of interest or at least some interest in these issues before entering the Riksdag; two said they had become interested, or more interested, after they had been members for some time. However, as noted above, nearly all started in other committees.

Some of the women thought it was difficult to get to work on these issues when they first entered the Riksdag. One said she realized that it would be hard to be nominated to the Standing Committee on Foreign Affairs, but still she tried. She thought that veteran members felt she was ill-advised to have asked for this Committee, and indeed she was not nominated to it then. It would be interesting to ascertain if new members of the Riksdag were ever posted to the Standing Committee on Foreign Affairs and if so, were men and women posted to the same extent?

_____

*Two of the women became deputy members of both another committee and of the Standing Committee on Foreign Affairs in one case and the Standing Committee on Defence in the other.

**The principle of appointing by seniority, or number of working years (see chapter I.A.3).

This woman was later appointed as a permanent member of the Standing Committee on Foreign Affairs. The reasons she perceived for her appointment are interesting. The appointment came after an election and a change of Government. Several men had left the Committee to become Cabinet ministers* and since she had by then been in the Riksdag for a long time, she was given a post in the Committee. When the Government changed again, the ruling party wanted the post of chairperson in this Committee and, at the same time, the party which this woman belonged to got the post of chairperson in another, less important committee. The woman then left the Standing Committee on Foreign Affairs and was appointed as chairperson in that other committee. This chain of events would seem to imply that only when important men had left the Committee was a woman able to enter and once they came back she was expected to leave, although she was given an important post in another committee.

Another woman also asked to join the Standing Committee on Foreign Affairs when she entered the Riksdag. She said she realized she was lucky to have got a post as deputy in this Committee. Her view of why she got the post was that not only were people being shuffled around in posts at that time, but there was also the need to have a woman on the Committee.

It seems that it was difficult for these women to get to work with these special issues. One woman did not mince words: if she had been a man, she said, she would have been allowed to deal with these issues at once, upon entering the Riksdag, but because she was a woman, this had been impossible.

One of the women who got to work on these issues after having been a member of the Riksdag for a time said she was asked to change both committee and issue. Apparently the party leader had wanted to shift people around into different committees after an election. One reason for having made this change was to place more men in committees dominated by women and to place more women in male-dominated committees. Two men said there was a conscious effort in their parties to elevate women to higher positions. This might indicate that the political parties are willing to adjust the participation of men and women to achieve more equal representation for both sexes in all the standing committees.

B. Women in important positions

When the interviewees were asked to name the most important positions in the areas of defence, disarmament, foreign affairs and foreign aid, that is, the positions in which a person would be best able to influence these issues, the following response emerged. The most influential posts were seen to be Minister for Foreign Affairs and Minister of Defence, which were regarded as equally important. The Under-Secretary of State for Foreign Affairs was also regarded as having a great deal of influence, more, in fact, than the Under-Secretary of State for Defence. The leaders of the main political parties, as well as the Prime Minister, were mentioned by over half of those interviewed.

The interviewees pointed out a few more influential posts: the Chairperson of the Delegation of Disarmament, the Supreme Commander of the Armed Forces, the Director-General of SIDA, the Minister of Foreign Aid, the Chairperson of the Standing Committee on Foreign Affairs, the head of the

---

*A member of the Riksdag is not allowed to be a member of a committee and a Cabinet minister at the same time.

Swedish Delegation to the Conference on Disarmament at Geneva, the head of the political department within the Ministry for Foreign Affairs and the Under-Secretary of State for Foreign Aid, within the Ministry for Foreign Affairs.

Some posts were mentioned by only one or two interviewees: the heads of the Defence, Army, Air and Naval Staffs, the Deputy Chairperson of the Standing Committee on Foreign Affairs, the Minister of Finance, some of the officials responsible for processing issues at the ministries concerned with foreign affairs and defence, the Minister of Foreign Trade, the Chairperson of the Defence Committee, the chairpersons of parliamentary committees on defence policy, that is, ministerial committees, some of the permanent members of the standing committees on foreign affairs and defence, the Speaker of the Riksdag, the Chairperson of the Swedish Delegation to the European Conference on Security and Co-operation and, finally, some experts at the National Defence Research Institute.

This list can now be examined to see how many of these important posts are currently held or have in the past been held by women. There has been one female Minister for Foreign Affairs and one female party leader, the same person. The chairpersonship of the Delegation of Disarmament has always been held by women. The Minister of Foreign Aid and the Minister of Foreign Trade were women in 1987. The post of Deputy Chairperson of the Standing Committee on Foreign Affairs was twice held by women, one of them the same person as held the post of Minister for Foreign Affairs. One or two members of the Standing Committee on Foreign Affairs and the Standing Committee on Defence, as well as of the officials with responsibility for processing issues at the two ministries, may have been women (they could have been either men or women, no names were given). It is abundantly clear that few important posts were held by women.

C. Obstacles and advantages

There were, in general, few women in the decision-making bodies dealing with defence, disarmament, foreign affairs and foreign aid. Moreover, as we saw above, there were even fewer women in the positions that are regarded as most important. The interviewees were asked what they thought were the reasons for this situation.

It is necessary at this point to distinguish between obstacles and indications of obstacles. While it would be difficult to identify actual obstacles, if there are any, it would not be so difficult to see signs of them. For example, if there are few women in high posts, it could be that something is preventing them from getting these posts. Here, the fact that few women are in high posts is a sign of possible obstacles, whereas the "something" is the obstacle itself. This study will point out some of the indications of obstacles. Further research would be needed to identify the obstacles themselves.

Factors that affect the indications of possible obstacles, as seen in chapter I and expressed and commented on by the persons interviewed, are discussed next, in chapter II.C.1. Advantages and disadvantages of being a woman, cited by the interviewed persons, are then discussed more in general in chapter II.C.2.

---

*See the introduction to chapter II.

1. Factors affecting the participation of women

Some factors that may be affecting the participation of women have been hypothesized to explain the data in chapter I. The interviewees were then asked for their comments on each of the hypotheses.

Importance of the position

One of the interviewees said that the reason there were few women in important positions was that women were generally only appointed to less important positions. According to her, the explanation was that only persons who were already important were appointed to other important positions. Many of those who made appointments thought by force of habit, this woman said. She pointed out that women who were able to do so, for example, female members of the Riksdag, should try to influence the persons who were doing the appointing and change their habits. Two other women said that the reason was prejudice. One of them added that traditions were strong: for example, public organizations nominate members to the boards of central governmental authorities; these nominees are then appointed by the Government. If only males are nominated in the first place, the Government has no choice but to appoint a male (see also chapter III).

These comments indicate that who is doing the appointing may have an influence on the participation of women. It would be interesting to know if women appoint women more often than men appoint women. The woman who had been Minister for Foreign Affairs said that when she held this post she tried to support women, and that some were appointed ambassadors.

In trying to explain why few women were chairpersons of standing committees of the Riksdag, some said the reason might be that women had on average been members of the Riksdag for shorter periods than men. Those who had been members of the Riksdag longest were indeed chosen for high positions. The principle of appointing by seniority was also cited by others being interviewed as a reason for the small number of women in high positions in the decision-making bodies of the Riksdag. As we saw, however, in chapter I.A.3, this cannot be the whole explanation, because women on average needed more years as members of the Riksdag than men to become chairpersons, but fewer years to become deputy chairpersons. One of the men interviewed thought that to get a post as chairperson one had to also be in a high position in the political party.

The interviews shed some additional light on the fact that women are more often appointed deputy members than permanent members of standing committees (see table 4). Some of the interviewees pointed out that there were occasionally more women than men at meetings of the Standing Committee on Foreign Affairs. According to them, this happened because deputy members often took over duties from permanent members, and these deputy members were likely to be women.

According to the people interviewed, when a party had more than one appointee in a committee, which was practically always the case, it gave some appointees precedence over others. Thus, the parties had their "first", "second" and "third" (for instance) members among both permanent and deputy members. These members often had different areas of competence* within the

---

*Although the political parties have different systems, often a member has an issue that is his or her special interest and responsibility.

issues handled by the committees. It could thus happen that a deputy member had the main responsibility for an issue within his or her party although he or she was only a deputy member of the committee.

This system influences the participation of women in two ways, the first, positive; the second, negative. Some of the interviewees pointed out that when issues of foreign aid and disarmament were discussed within the Standing Committee on Foreign Affairs, women were not underrepresented. Indeed, the people who had the responsibility for these issues within the parties were often women, they said. For example, of the four political parties represented,* three had entrusted women with the responsibility for disarmament issues. However, this system was also claimed to influence the participation of women negatively. Another of the interviewees said that women were often the "last" permanent members, that is the lowest in the scale of precedence, which meant that they were the ones who had to leave first if the party lost seats in an election. She said that this had happened in her own party after one election, but that the situation had changed since then. In reply to the question of why women were very often the "last" permanent members, she said she thought it was because of appointment by seniority. Obviously, it is commonly thought that this principle influences appointments to all positions, not only to high positions.

Importance of the decision-making body

The participation of women seems to be negatively correlated with the importance of the decision-making body, although not as much so as with the importance of the position. Just as the interviewees were asked to name the most important positions, they were also asked to name the decision-making bodies that were most important from a political standpoint. The most important were held to be the Advisory Council on Foreign Affairs and the Standing Committee on Foreign Affairs, followed by the parliamentary committees on defence policy (ministerial committees) and the Standing Committee on Defence.

Other decision-making bodies were also mentioned, for example, the Delegation of Disarmament, the Government, the executives of the political parties, the Ministry for Foreign Affairs, in particular its political department, the Ministry of Defence, the board of SIDA and the Riksdag as a whole.

Female participation in these bodies has not been markedly lower than in the remaining decision-making bodies examined. Of the bodies mentioned above as being important, the Parliamentary Committee on Defence Policy (a ministerial committee), the Advisory Council on Foreign Affairs and the Ministry of Defence had the lowest female participation in 1986/87, approximately 15 per cent. In the other bodies mentioned above, female participation was higher. The Advisory Council on Foreign Affairs and the Standing Committee on Foreign Affairs were regarded as very important, which is interesting insofar as neither can formally make decisions (see chapter I.A.1).

---

*The Swedish Social Democratic Party, the Centre Party, the Liberal Party and the Moderate Party.

Focusing on the membership of these decision-making bodies, it can be seen that one person is often a member of more than one body. Both men and women who already hold important positions seem to get other important positions. This tendency is exemplified by the composition of the War Delegation.* It would, however, be interesting to see if there is any difference between men and women in regard to this.

One particular department within the Ministry for Foreign Affairs, the political department, was thought to be especially important. When the proportions of women in all departments of this Ministry in 1986/87 were compared, it could be seen that the political department had the smallest proportion. Within that department 9 per cent were women, while within the administrative and juridical departments 41 per cent and 51 per cent were women, respectively. 26/

Issue dealt with by the decision-making body

With respect to the decision-making bodies examined here, it seems that it was most difficult for women to achieve equal representation in bodies that dealt with defence issues. Different explanations have been offered for this phenomenon (see chapter I).

Some issues can be regarded as more important than others. One of the people being interviewed said she thought that women were appointed to issues of lesser importance and, accordingly, to less important decision-making bodies, as discussed above. She also compared issues concerning defence, disarmament and foreign affairs with all other issues. She said that women had difficulties in getting to work with defence issues because they had not, for example, done military service, a view that was shared by one of the men interviewed. Because they were less interested in technical matters than men and because they had not done military service, women were not familiar with different weapons, which was a disadvantage if they wanted to work with these issues.

When the various issues are being talked about they are often characterized as "soft" or "hard". There are, however, differences in what the interviewees think of as soft and hard and there are also different opinions as to why women are more often involved in issues that are thought of as soft.

Some of the people interviewed characterized as soft those issues having to do with daily life, such as children and care of the elderly, consumer policy, culture, education, nursing and environmental issues. Hard issues were those issues that had to do with technology, the economy and defence. One person thought it was indeed true that women worked with soft issues while the men worked with hard ones. This situation, she said, has been brought about by men, who made sure that women got to work only with these issues. Another believed that women were assigned to these not-so-difficult issues because that was what had always been done. Her feeling was, however, that this had changed somewhat.

One of the interviewees thought the situation was attributable to different backgrounds and experiences. Most women still had the main responsibility for home and children, and this made it natural for them to

---

*The War Delegation has no importance in peacetime. However, in the event of war or danger of war, it takes over the duties of the Riksdag and then becomes very important (see chapter I.A.3).

work with, for example, education. This point of view was shared by another woman. She added, however, that it was often chance that decided what issue a politician was going to work with.

The interviewees were asked to rank defence, disarmament, foreign affairs and foreign aid on a hard-soft scale. Two of them did not want to make such a ranking, because they thought it was impossible; five did not know where to put foreign affairs on such a scale; and two did not know where to put foreign aid.

Defence issues, they said, were hard or very hard. Some of them mentioned the export of weapons as a very hard issue. The other issues were not as hard as defence, but the interviewees did not agree on which was the softest. The one they disagreed about most was disarmament. Three thought that it was soft or very soft, five thought it of middling hardness, while two others thought it was hard. Foreign affairs was said to be hard but not as hard as defence. Some pointed out that foreign affairs was difficult to classify because it had so many ingredients, some of them hard, others not. Foreign aid was regarded by some of the people interviewed as a part of foreign affairs; one said it was a hard issue, while six said it was soft.

The results of this exercise are interesting, especially since the interviewees disagreed about disarmament issues. While disarmament was regarded by many as a women's issue, not everyone regarded it as soft. It was a common mistake for an issue to be classified as soft simply because women worked with it and not because the issue itself was soft. In addition, disarmament was a relatively new issue, and it is perhaps for this reason that the interviewees disagreed so much about its softness/hardness.

Size of the decision-making body

It could be seen that the total number of persons in nearly all the decision-making bodies increased; in only a few bodies did their number decline. It seems, moreover, that the total number of people in a body influenced the participation of women. In those cases where the total number declined, the percentage share of female participants declined also, indicating that it was the women who were leaving and also that more women were given posts when the total number of posts was increasing. This finding is interesting and warrants further research. None of the interviewees commented on this factor.

Visibility of the decision-making body

The interviewees attributed differences in female participation to other factors as well. One person said that the visibility of the authority had an effect on the participation of women. Political parties were bound to have women candidates on the ballot, because the electorate would notice this. Within the Riksdag and the ministerial committees, however, the relative proportions of men and women were no longer highly visible to the public, so few women got high posts, or indeed any posts, in these bodies, according to this woman.

Another woman said that when directly elected persons, that is, members of the Riksdag, elect persons to indirectly appointed decision-making bodies, the participation of women suffered.

Another variable is whether the members of the decision-making bodies are members of the Riksdag or officials. As was seen in chapter I, female participation in Swedish delegations abroad was higher if the delegates were members of the Riksdag rather than officials.

2. Possible advantages of being a woman

While this discussion focuses on how the interviewees felt about women within the issues of defence, disarmament, foreign affairs and foreign aid and asks them if women are blocked in one way or another, it also raises the question whether it is an advantage to be a woman.

Opinions varied on this matter. Two women thought they were elected members of the Riksdag partly because they were women. The need for female politicians was great, one of them said. One of the people interviewed felt that the electorate consciously votes for a slate of candidates headed by a female. One of the women believed that she had been appointed to the Standing Committee on Foreign Affairs because she was a woman.

One woman thought there were both advantages and disadvantages to being a woman. On the one hand, a matter sometimes became more interesting when a woman took it up. On the other hand, women were not given serious consideration when an important position was being filled.

One of the interviewees, saying she had had no problems when working with disarmament issues and also speaking for other women who have worked with this issue, gave two reasons: first, she had already had a political position when she started to work with this issue and, secondly, she had more knowledge than the men thought she had. She added, however, that she had experienced some resistance because she was a woman, both in her political career and as a member of the Parliamentary Committee on Defence Policy, a ministerial committee. But she also thought that this resistance was less than it would once have been, a belief that was echoed by another woman.

The interviewees thought that men and women participated on an equal footing in the work of the Riksdag. A number of those interviewed said that men's and women's contributions to debates were taken equally seriously. Some of the men thought that women found it more difficult than men to combine the roles of parent and member of the Riksdag. They thought that men generally believed women should take care of the home and children, even if they were members of the Riksdag. The male members of the Riksdag, by contrast, did not have this disadvantage: they thought it natural for their wives to take care of the home.

The interviewees suggested other disadvantages and obstacles. One woman thought there were few women in decision-making bodies for two reasons. First, women had always had a hard time getting appointed to decision-making bodies and, secondly, there was hidden resistance to women. One woman remarked that it was often the woman who had to stay home if, for example, the children were sick. She also thought, however, that the law giving both mothers and fathers the right to stay home with the children was very important for women's chances to get to work within decision-making bodies.

One of the women interviewed said that the media, including television and radio, concentrated on party leaders, which was a disadvantage for women because the party leaders were often men. Another when she, as a female member of the Riksdag, was out campaigning or giving speeches she had to justify being there, whereas a male member did not. She added that this was a problem that had become more pronounced in recent years. She found it was taken for granted that a man would know about defence issues, while a woman would have to prove that she knew. Another woman who had also worked with defence issues claimed that a woman gained respect if she was really knowledgeable on these issues and that it could then actually be an advantage to be a woman. The same feeling was expressed by another woman, who said that there were advantages to being a woman, because as a woman one had to have more knowledge about an issue, and well-informed people were always appreciated. The need to have more knowledge than a man could of course be an obstacle, she pointed out. One of the men thought it was very important that women not need to have more knowledge than men to get high positions.

All these women felt was that if they had been men, people would have paid more attention to their views. One said that she thought this was especially the case when working in a male-dominated issue.

Some of the interviewed women said that it was still difficult to be a female politician, although they emphasized that this was not always true. One woman said that in the Delegation of Disarmament, for example, there was no difference between men and women. She felt, as did one of the other women, that the obstacles lay, instead, within the political party. One of them thought that men were very eager to achieve high positions, while the other said she had experienced resistance to getting to work with these issues, i.e. defence, disarmament, foreign affairs and foreign aid. Conversely, one of the other women said she had never met any obstacles within her party.

When asked if they had faced any obstacles when working with defence, disarmament, foreign affairs and foreign aid, women replied that they did not feel that they had been blocked, either when working with these issues in general or when working within the party's parliamentary group. One of them believed that in Sweden it had long been accepted for women to work with these issues. She pointed especially to the work of Alva Myrdal and Inga Thorsson.

Some of the women who had worked with these issues outside Sweden, for example as members of the Swedish Delegation to the European Council, said that equal representation had been much more nearly achieved in the Nordic countries than in the other countries of Europe. One of the women thought that citizens of the Nordic countries did not have to work for equal representation in their own countries as it was already very good, and that the small difference in representation would solve itself. The big problem was to get equal representation internationally, she thought. She thought that she and other Swedish women who had worked with these issues internationally had not felt any resistance; rather, they felt being a woman had been an advantage. Another woman said that she, too, thought there was a larger gap in other countries between the proportions of men and women in decision-making bodies.

D. Rationale for including more women

The question of why it is important to include more women will now be dealt with. The interviewees were asked what they thought and if they had any recommendations. One of them said it was important for men and women to live on equal terms, and that practical opportunities must be created. Since these opportunities were built on equality, it was important that decision-making bodies represented the whole population, she argued. Other women as well as some of the men argued along those same lines: women represented half of the population and had different experiences from men. One of them added that it was necessary to get more men into female-dominated fields.

Their different experiences led men and women to take different approaches, another woman believed. She said that women usually took a holistic approach to the issues that concerned society, while men had a more fragmented approach. Politicians had to realize that it was very important to include women in decision-making bodies because of this difference in approach, she added. One of the men thought that decisions might be different if there were more women in decision-making bodies.

The different approaches of men and women were especially obvious when it came to environmental issues and peace and security issues, two of the inter- viewees thought. Although some men were active in these issues, more than one interviewee believed that it was important to get more men active in them and that it was important also to let men take care of children, because this affected their approaches. It was also a question of equal opportunities: if men were given the chance to be at home, it would be easier for women to get to work within decision-making bodies.

While a number of those interviewed thought women and men had different approaches, only one said that this was due to biological differences. The rest said that the differences depended mainly on variations in background and experience. One pointed out that women had no military traditions and thought that this affected their approaches; conversely, another felt that military experts did not think any differently from herself. Two women did not think there was any difference in approaches between men and women. One thought that women in decision-making positions would make more peaceable decisions than men, and she also believed that if more women had been involved in disarmament negotiations there would have been better results.

One of the men thought it would be good to have a feminine pattern of reaction in respect of, for example, disarmament issues. He thought that if women, because of their closer contact with children and their closer relation- ship to questions of survival, had been more able to influence conflicts, armaments and the development of the society in general, there would have been fewer tensions and the world would have been less dominated by conflict.

One of the interviewees thought that work within the decision-making bodies would be benefited if there was equal representation. Two of the women thought that the number of women was important, as it was hard for a few women to have an impact. One of them disagreed with the argument that it was hard to find women who were qualified enough. More than one of the women argued that if those who made appointments took the trouble to look for women, they would find them.

The interviewees were asked if there had been situations where all the women in a decision-making body had had a common view contrary to that of all the men. Generally speaking, the answer was no, and it was explained that the most important divisions were between the political parties and not between men and women. It had happened, however, on one or two occasions, that in special women's issues all the women had held the same opinion. One woman asked a rhetorical question: if women had a majority in the Riksdag, would they use it to overrule the men? She thought they might do this in women's issues, but not in general.

With respect to what should be done to remedy the unequal representation of men and women, two women and one man wanted to have quotas in one form or another, while one woman said that quotas could be tried but ought not to be necessary. Of the remaining eight people, three women and three men said they did not want to have quotas, while two women thought that other means could be used.

E. Summary

Female representation in the decision-making bodies studied can be said to be influenced by the importance of the position, the importance of the body, the issues being dealt with, the total number of persons in the decision-making body and the visibility of the body.

Opinions diverged about possible obstacles for women as well as possible advantages. Overall, both women and men thought there were some obstacles; women, on the other hand, also felt that sometimes it was advantageous to have been a woman.

On the question of how to achieve equal representation in decision-making bodies, some men and women wanted to have quotas, while others did not.

III. CONCLUSIONS AND RECOMMENDATIONS

On the basis of this pilot study, it is possible to draw some preliminary conclusions and to make recommendations for research and action, both immediate and long-term, to increase the representation of women in the decision-making processes related to peace and disarmament. The recommendations are directed to the United Nations and Governments, but some of these recommendations could also apply to such groups as academic researchers, political parties, pressure groups and non-governmental organizations.

The chances for women of increasing their participation in decision-making seem to be greater when nominations, appointments and elections draw from a wide base and are conducted in line with democratic principles according to clear formulae. The larger the pool of potential candidates is, the greater are the chances of women's access to decision-making positions. Informal recruitment from a small group works to their disadvantage.

Women are more likely to be included in a decision-making body when it is highly visible and its operation is transparent. Conversely, when the decision-making structure of a group has low visibility, the recruitment and appointment rules are unclear or secret, or there is considerable co-option, their participation is less likely.

Women in Swedish decision-making bodies are frequently in secondary positions, that is, they are often deputy members and lower in the hierarchy than men. While it is important that a decision-making body has an equal number of women and men, it is perhaps more important that women and men have equal authority and power within such bodies.

While the effect of methods of recruitment and appointment on the participation of women has not been studied in detail, the informal principle of appointment by seniority to important committees may work against female parliamentarians. Those who do the appointing often are not aware of, or may not wish to be aware of, suitable women. Research needs to be carried out on the behaviour of women who already hold high positions to ascertain whether they appoint more women than their male counterparts and, if so, whether this is a conscious policy.

A research issue to consider is the extent to which changes in the base for recruitment has an effect on female representation. For example, a study of the careers of women officers would be useful in terms of promotion within the military hierarchy and involvement in defence policy issues. A recommended parallel study would be whether a background in the peace movement is considered as a positive factor in access to formal decision-making on defence issues.

Increases in the total number of people in a decision-making body has some bearing on the representation of women; as the total number increases, the proportion of female representation also increases.

Other factors also account for the differences between women's involvement in defence and international affairs and in disarmament and foreign aid. For example, women may find it easier to get positions in bodies that deal with new issues, and disarmament and foreign aid could be said to be newer issues than defence and foreign affairs. However, it is difficult for new issues to

receive the same support as conventional ones, especially budgeting support.
It is recommended that a study be done on whether issues associated with women
are allocated the same resources as those in which men predominate and whether
new issues, once women become involved, begin to lose their share of resources.

Regardless of the visibility of a decision-making body, its real
political importance determines the level of participation of women in it.
While the body for political importance has not been examined, it seems that
the most visible and the least politically important bodies have the largest
proportions of women. Real power may not lie in the formal decision-making
bodies, however; in Sweden there seems to be considerable overlapping of
responsibilities, which is an issue that should be considered more carefully.
Women can also gain positions of apparent or actual power in politically
important decision-making bodies even if these bodies are not publicly
visible. However, it would be useful to examine whether decision-making power
shifts between these bodies in such cases.

It seems that when the members of a body are not directly elected, but
are co-opted by those who have been elected, women are often underrepresented.
In this sense also, democracy would promote the cause of women. A more
equitable representation of men and women in the Riksdag ought therefore to
serve as a model for other decision-making bodies. It might be suggested, for
example, that all of them should have at least 40 per cent female membership.

Obstacles that impede women from working with peace and disarmament
issues are difficult to pinpoint. It is difficult to get positions in the
Standing Committee on Foreign Affairs or the Standing Committee on Defence.
In issues traditionally associated with men, women have to prove their
knowledge before being accepted. Indeed, they often are required to have
more knowledge than men.

A basic issue is whether it is desirable to have equal participation of
women with men in decision-making bodies and whether that would make a
qualitative difference in the policies adopted. There are two factors to
consider. First, it is a matter of democratic principle in that men and women
should participate to the same degree in decision-making. Sweden has
universal and equal suffrage, but men and women do not seem to have the same
opportunity to influence the political decisions made between elections. 27/

Secondly, resource-allocation decisions, if they are to be efficacious
and just, should take into account the different experiences of men and women
and their different values and interests. If the views of women are excluded,
as seems to be the case, their important shared knowledge and experience is
also lost.

The United Nations and Governments should, therefore, continue to analyse
the representation of women in decision-making processes related to peace and
disarmament at national, regional and global levels, as a basis for practical
action. While the methodology and techniques will inevitably vary from
country to country, the focus should remain on the quality of women, and their
participation and influence in decision-making processes rather than their
number. Some recommendations on how to undertake this analysis are given
below.

The case-study on Sweden covers two stages of the decision-making process, the formal decisions and their implementation. Other parts of the process must also be studied in order to arrive at a more thorough and realistic assessment of female participation in decisions that affect peace and disarmament. In Sweden, for example, democratic and open political discussion reveal a great deal in formal decision-making, but other stages of the decision-making process also merit attention: pressure groups, political parties, public and academic debate can all be influential. In societies that have more informal, hidden power structures, other methods might be needed to assess female participation.

The role of the media can be examined from a number of perspectives: the number of women journalists writing on peace and disarmament; the relative number of articles being written about women in peace and disarmament issues; other women academics formulate research programmes; and the number of female researchers working with questions of peace and disarmament.

An important subject is the role of women in relevant organizations, governmental and non-governmental, especially in the formulation and implementation of their programmes. The effect of non-governmental organizations on final decisions at the national level should be assessed. For example, a potential area of inquiry would be the participation and influence of women in trade unions. In countries that have institutes such as, in Sweden, the equality ombudsman (JämO) and the office of Equal Opportunity within the Ministry of Labour, these bodies could be surveyed to see if they have encountered complaints of women being prevented or discouraged from undertaking peace-related work.

The study of political parties is particularly important. In Sweden, the representation of women in the parties in the Riksdag and in the Government has been described. However, the functions of a political party extend beyond these institutions: it can play a role at all levels of society.

The nature of the participation of women in all stages of the decision-making process must be examined. It should be established how questions of peace and disarmament are considered at different levels of decision-making bodies and how the processes whereby decisions on peace and desarmament are made.

The extent to which the representation of women differs from one issue to another and whether those issues associated with women attract the same share of resources as those associated with men should be examined. It is crucial to ascertain whether the policies of decision-making bodies change once the representation of men and women is equal and once women are in decision-making positions.

Notes

1/ Statistics Sweden, Women and Men in Sweden: Facts and Figures, Equal Opportunity, Know Your Facts, 1985 (Stockholm, Statistics Sweden (SCB), 1985), p. 1 (hereinafter referred to as Women and Men in Sweden).

2/ Ibid.

3/ Women and Men in Sweden ..., p. 4; Statistics Sweden, Kvinno- och Mansvär(1)den: fakta om jämställheten i Sverige 1986 (Stockholm, Norstedts Tryckeri, 1986), p. 169 (hereinafter referred to as Kvinno-och Mansvär(1)den).

4/ <u>Women and Men in Sweden</u> ..., pp. 4-5.

5/ Central Services Office for the Ministries, <u>Handlingsprogram för jämställdhet i regeringskansliet</u>, 1986, p. 11 (hereinafter referred to as <u>Handlingsprogram</u>).

6/ <u>Constitutional Documents of Sweden</u>, The Instrument of Government, chap. 10.

7/ <u>Ibid</u>., The Instrument of Government, chap. 13, and the Riksdag Act, chap. 8; A. Halvarsson, <u>Sveriges statsskick: en faktasamling</u> (Stockholm, Esselte Studium, 1977), pp. 11 and 76.

8/ <u>Norstedts Uppslagsbok</u> (Stockholm, Norstedt and Söners Förlag, 1982), p. 911.

9/ B. Sundelius, ed., <u>Foreign Policies of Northern Europe</u> (Boulder, Colorado, Westview Press, 1982), p. 135.

10/ <u>Sveriges Statskalender 1977</u> (Stockholm, Liber Allmänna Förlaget, 1977), p. 354.

11/ Central Services Office for Parliament, <u>Fakta om Folkvalda: Riksdagen 1985-1988</u> (Stockholm, Central Services Office for Parliament, 1986), pp. 325-332; <u>Kvinno- och Mansvär(1)den</u> ..., p. 172.

12/ P. Vinde and G. Petri, <u>Swedish Government Administration: an Introduction</u>, 2nd rev. ed. (Stockholm, Prisma/The Swedish Institute, 1978), p. 17.

13/ B. Molin, L. Mansson and L. Strömberg, <u>Offentlig förvaltning: Stats- och kommunalförvaltningens struktur och funktioner</u> (Stockholm, BonnierFakta Bokförlag, 1982), pp. 63-65 (hereinafter referred to as <u>Offentlig förvaltning</u>).

14/ <u>Kvinno- och Mansvär(1)den</u> ..., p. 170.

15/ <u>Handlingsprogram</u> ..., pp. 4 and 9.

16/ <u>Handlingsprogram</u> ..., pp. 2-3.

17/ <u>Fakta om Folkvalda</u> ..., pp. 335-336.

18/ <u>Ibid</u>.

19/ Ministry of Labour, <u>Ska även morgondagens samhälle formas enbart av män?</u> DsA 1986:4 (Stockholm, Regeringskansliets Offsetcentral, 1986), pp. 26-27.

20/ <u>Ibid</u>., pp. 27-28.

21/ <u>Kvinno- och Mansvär(1)den</u> ..., p. 172.

22/ <u>Ibid</u>., p. 173. See also appendix 2B, tables 1 and 2.

23/ <u>Offentlig förvaltning</u> ..., pp. 69-70.

24/ <u>Ibid</u>., p. 39 and pp. 72-73.

- 58 -

25/ <u>Ska även morgondagens samhälle formas enbart av män?</u>, p. 20 and 107.

26/ Sveriges Statskalender 1986 (Stockholm, Liber Allmänna Förlaget, 1986), pp. 59-63.

27/ Ministry of Labour, <u>Varannan damernas</u>, Final report of the Committee on Women's Representation (Stockholm, Svenskt Tryck, 1987), pp. 51-55.

28/ <u>Ibid</u>., p. 161.

Annex

SUMMARY TABLE OF ALL THE DECISION-MAKING BODIES INCLUDED IN THE STUDY

THE MAIN DECISION-MAKING BODY	DECISION-MAKING BODIES AFTER ISSUE: (A) GENERAL ISSUES	No of table	DECISION-MAKING BODIES DEALING WITH: (B) DEFENCE ISSUES	No of table	(C) DISARMAMENT ISSUES	No of table	(D) FOREIGN AFFAIRS/AID.	No of table	APPENDIX
(1) THE PARLIAMENT (THE RIKSDAG)	Parliament as a whole	<A1.1>	Parliamentary Standing Committee on Defence	<B1.1>	(1)		Parliamentary Standing Committee on Foreign Affairs	<D1.1>	APP. 1
	Advisory Council on Foreign Affairs	<A1.2>							
	Sw. War Delegation	<A1.3>							
	Sw. Deleg. to the Nordic Council	<A1.4>							
	Executive Comm. of Riksdag Interparl. Group	<A1.5>							
(2) THE GOVERNMENT	Government as a whole	<A2.1>	Ministry of Defence	<B2.1>	(1)		Ministry for Foreign Affairs	<D2.1>	APP. 2A & 2B
	Office of the Prime Minister	<A2.2>	Ministerial Committees subordinated to the Ministry of Defence (B2.2.1 - B2.2.23)	<B2.2>			Ministerial Committees subordinated to the Ministry for Foreign Affairs (D2.2.1 - D2.2.14)	<D2.2>	
(3) THE CENTRAL GOVERNMENT AUTHORITIES			THE FOLLOWING DECISION-MAKING BODIES ARE SUBORDINATED TO THE MINISTRY OF DEFENCE:		THE FOLLOWING DECISION-MAKING BODIES ARE SUBORDINATED TO THE MINISTRY FOR FOREIGN AFFAIRS:		THE FOLLOWING DECISION-MAKING BODIES ARE SUBORDINATED TO THE MINISTRY FOR FOREIGN AFFAIRS:		APPENDIX 3A
			Supreme Commander of the Armed Forces and Defence Staff	<B3.1>	The Delegation of Disarmament	<C3.1>	Sw. International Humanitarian Law Delegation	<D3.1>	
			The Head of the Army and Army Staff	<B3.2>			Sw. International Development Authority (SIDA)	<D3.2>	
			The Head of the National Home Guard and the National Home Guard Staff	<B3.3>			Sw. Board for Education in Internat. Development	<D3.3>	
			The Head of the Navy and the Naval Staff	<B3.4>			Consultative Committee on Humanitarian Assistance	<D3.4>	
			The Head of the Air Forces and the Air Staff	<B3.5>			Advisory Council on Develop. Cooper. Issues	<D3.5>	&
			Defence Materiel Administration (FMV)	<B3.6>			Diplomatic Service & Delegations:		
			THE FOLLOWING DECISION-MAKING BODIES ARE SUBORDINATED TO MIN. OF DEFENCE BUT ARE NOT INCL. IN THE ARMED FORCES:				Ambassadors	<D3.6.1>	APPENDIX 3B
			National Board of Civil Defence	<B3.7>			Permanent Mission of Sweden to the UN, New York.	<D3.7.1A>	
			National Board for Rescue and Fire Services				Sw. Permanent Mission to Internat. Org. in Geneva	<D3.7.1B>	
			National Board of Psychological Defence	<B3.8>			Sw. Del. to the Conference on Disarmament in Geneva	<D3.7.1C>	
			National Board of Economic Defence	<B3.9>			Sw. Del. to European Conf. of Security & Cooper.	<D3.7.2>	
			Office of the Director, Regional Civilian Defence Areas	<B3.10>			Sw. Delegations to the UN General Ass., 1st Comm.	<D3.7.3>	
							Two special Sessions of UN Gen. Ass. of Disarmament	<D3.7.4>	
							Sw. Del to World Conf. of Disarmament & Development, UN	<D3.7.5>	

(1) There is no specific disarmament-issue body in parliament or government. Disarmament issues are dealt with in the Standing Committee on Foreign Affairs and the Ministry for Foreign Affairs, respectively.

INFORMATION - SUMMARY TABLE

The table above summarizes the decision-making bodies included in this study. Chapters 2.1 - 2.3 corresponds to the main decision-making bodies marked as 1, 2 and 3, in column one. The second column includes those bodies which deal with defence, disarmament and foreign affairs/aid, that is, general-issue bodies. The following columns include the bodies which deal with defence issues; disarmament issues and foreign affairs/aid, respectively. Column 2-5 are marked with A, B, C, D. This reference system is used throughout the Appendices. In Appendix 1 you will find the decision-making bodies within parliament, in Appendix 2A bodies within the Government Office, Appendix 2B the ministerial committees, in Appendix 3A the central government authorities and finally in Appendix 3B you will find the Diplomatic Service and delegations. First in each chapters there are some tables, summarizing each Appendix and/or tables with special information.

Appendix 1

Statistical Data of the Representation of Women in Decision-Making Bodies within the Swedish Parliament (the Riksdag).

Table 1: The Parliamentary Standing Committees.

Table 1a: The 10 Parliamentary Standing Committees 1966/67.
Chairperson and Deputy Chairperson by sex.

Standing Committee	Chairperson (Sex)	Deputy Chairperson (Sex)
1. Standing Committee on the Constitution (Konstitutionsutsk.)	Man	Man
2. 1st Standing Committee on Civil-Law Legislation (Första lagutsk.)	Woman	Man
3. 2nd Standing Committee on Civil-Law Legislation (Andra lagutsk.)	Man	Man
4. 3dr Standing Committee on Civil-Law Legislation (Tredje lagutsk.)	Man	Man
5. Standing Committee on Foreign Affairs (Utrikesutsk.)	Man	Man
6. Standing Committee on Agriculture (Jordbruksutsk.)	Man	Man
7. Standing Committee on Banking and Currency (Bankoutsk.)	Man	Man
8. Standing Committee of Ways and Means (Bevillningsutsk.)	Man	Man
9. Standing Committee of Supply (Statsutsk.)⋆	Man	Man
10. Standing Committee on Miscellaneous Affairs (Allm. beredn.utsk.)	Woman	Man

⋆ See footnote below table B1.1a, App. 1, page 6.

Source: Sveriges Statskalender 1967, page 251-259 (Jan 1967).

Table 1b: The 16 Parliamentary Standing Committiees 1976/77 and 1986/87.
Chairperson and Deputy Chairperson by sex.

Standing Committee on	Chairperson (Sex)		Deputy Chairperson (Sex)	
	76/77	86/87	76/77	86/87
1. Constitution (Konst.utsk.)	Man	Man	Man	Man
2. Finance (Finansutsk.)	Man	Man	Man	Man
3. Taxation (Skatteutsk.)	Man	Man	Man	Man
4. Justice (Justitieusk.)	Woman	Woman	Woman	Man
5. Civil-Law Legislation (Lagutsk.)	Man	Man	Man	Man
6. Foreign Affairs (Utrikesutsk.)	Man	Man	Woman	Woman
7. Defence (Försvarsutsk.)	Man	Man	Man	Man
8. Social Insurance (Socialförs.utsk.)	Man	Woman	Man	Man
9. Social Questions (Socialutsk.)	Man	Man	Man	Man
10. Cultural Affairs (Kulturutsk.)	Man	Woman	Man	Woman
11. Education (Utbildningsutsk.)	Man	Man	Man	Man
12. Agriculture (Jordbruksutsk.)	Man	Man	Man	Man
13. Transport and Communications (Trafikutsk.)	Man	Man	Man	Man
14. Industry and Commerce (Näringsutsk.)	Man	Man	Man	Man
15. Labour Market (Arbetsmarkn.utsk.)	Man	Man	Man	Man
16. Physical Planning and Local Government Only 1976/77 (Civilutsk.)	Man	-	Man	-
16. Housing. Only 1986/87 (Bostadsutsk.)	-	Man	-	Man

Source: Sveriges Statskalender 1977, page 344-345 (Jan 1977).
Sveriges Statskalender 1986, page 53-54 (Jan 1986).

Table 2: Members of the 16 Parliamentary Standing Committees. March 1, 1986.

Table 2a: Permanent Members of the 16 Parliamentary Standing Committees by sex.‡ March 1, 1986.
Ranked after Female Participation.

Standing Committee on	Number of		Percent	
	Women	Men	Women	Men
Cultural Affairs	9[1,2]	6	60%	40%
Social Insurance	9[1]	6	60%	40%
Social Questions	7	8	47%	53%
Civil-Law Legislation	5	10	33%	67%
Justice	4[1]	11	27%	73%
Foreign Affairs	4[2]	11	27%	73%
Labour Market	4	11	27%	73%
Education	4	11	27%	73%
Housing	3	12	20%	80%
Finance	3	12	20%	80%
Defence	3	12	20%	80%
Agriculture	3	12	20%	80%
Constitution	3	12	20%	80%
Industry and Commerce	3	12	20%	80%
Taxation	2	13	13%	87%
Transport and Communications	2	13	13%	87%
TOTAL	68	172	28%	72%

‡ The total number of Permanent
Members is always 15.
[1] The Chairperson is a woman.
[2] The Deputy Chairperson is a woman.

Table 2b: Deputy Members of the 16 Parliamentary Standing Committees, by sex‡. March 1, 1986.
Ranked after Female Participation.

Standing Committee on	Number of		Percent	
	Women	Men	Women	Men
Social Insurance	9	6	60%	40%
Constitution	9	9	50%	50%
Social Questions	8	8	50%	50%
Civil-Law Legislation	7	8	47%	53%
Cultural Affairs	8	10	44%	56%
Education	7	10	41%	59%
Foreign Affairs	7	13	35%	65%
Finance	6	12	33%	67%
Defence	6	12	33%	67%
Transport and Communications	5	10	33%	67%
Justice	5	10	33%	67%
Housing	5	11	31%	69%
Labour Market	6	14	30%	70%
Taxation	5	12	29%	71%
Industry and Commerce	4	15	21%	79%
Agriculture	2	16	11%	89%
TOTAL	99	176	36%	64%

‡ The total number of Deputy Members is
at least 15. The number is not the
same in all committees.

Source, table 2a and 2b: Central Services Office for the Riksdag, "Fakta om folkvalda. Riksdagen 1985
- 1988", page 325-332.

Table 3: Per Cent Female Member (Number of Women) in Each Party in 1966/67, First and Second Chamber[1].

Political Party	First Chamber	Second Chamber	Both Chambers	Men and Women. Total Number. Both Chambers.
(m)	12% (3)	15% (5)	14% (8)	59
(c)	5% (1)	0% (1)	2% (1)	54
(fp)	8% (2)	7% (5)	7% (5)	68
(s)	12% (10)	22% (25)	18% (35)	193
(vpk)	0% (0)	11% (1)	11% (1)	9
All Parties	11% (16)	15% (34)	13% (50)	
Members of Parliament (total number)	151	233		384[2]

[1] For some information about the change from two to one chamber, see footnote below table A1.1 in Appendix 1.
[2] A party called Medborgerlig Samling had one member (a man) in the second chamber.

Source: Riksdagsmatrikel 1967, Part I, page 30 and Part II, page 43. (Jan 1967)

SUMMARY OF DECISION-MAKING BODIES - THE PARLIAMENT (THE RIKSDAG).

TABLE 4: Number of and Per Cent Women of Permanent and Deputy Members, by Year.

NAME OF DECISION-MAKING BODY	NUMBER OF WOMEN			PER CENT WOMEN			TOTAL NUMBER OF MEMBERS**			No of table
	1966/67	1976/77	1986/87	1966/67	1976/77	1986/87	1966/67	1976/77	1986/87	
The Parliament as a whole (Riksdag)	50	80	113	13%	23%	32%	384	349	349	(A1.1)
Advisory Council on Foreign Affairs	3	3	4	9%	13%	17%	33	23	23	(A1.2)
War Delegation	6	6	3	12%	12%	18%	51	51	51	(A1.3)
Su. Del. to the Nordic Council	4	3	16	12%	25%	40%	32	36	40	(A1.4)
Executive Committee of the Riksdag										
Interparliamentary Group	2	6	6	13%	38%	38%	15	16	16	(A1.5)
Standing Committee on Defence	1	5	3	6%	16%	26%	18	31	34	(B1.1)
Standing Comm. on Foreign Affairs	3	7	12	9%	23%	33%	32	31	36	(D1.1)
ALL DECISION-MAKING BODIES	69	116	169	12%	22%	31%	565	537	549	
THE RIKSDAG NOT INCLUDED	19	36	56	10%	19%	28%	181	188	200	

* The whole Parliament and the War Delegation only includes permanent members.
** Both men and women.

TABLE 5: Number of and Per Cent Women of Permanent Members, by Year.

NAME OF DECISION-MAKING BODY	NUMBER OF WOMEN			PER CENT WOMEN			TOTAL NUMBER OF MEMBERS*		
	1966/67	1976/77	1986/87	1966/67	1976/77	1986/87	1966/67	1976/77	1986/87
The Parliament as a whole (Riksdag)	50	80	113	13%	23%	32%	384	349	349
Advisory Council on Foreign Affairs	1	2	2	6%	18%	22%	17	11	11
War Delegation	6	6	9	12%	12%	18%	51	51	51
Su. Del. to the Nordic Council	3	3	7	19%	17%	35%	16	18	20
Executive Committee of the Riksdag									
Interparliamentary Group	1	5	2	11%	56%	22%	9	9	9
Standing Committee on Defence	1	2	5	6%	13%	20%	6	15	15
Standing Comm. on Foreign Affairs	1	5	5	6%	33%	33%	16	15	15
ALL DECISION-MAKING BODIES	63	103	141	13%	22%	30%	439	468	470
THE RIKSDAG NOT INCLUDED	13	23	28	11%	19%	23%	115	119	121

* Both men and women.

TABLE 6: Number of and Per Cent Women of Deputy Members, by Year.

NAME OF DECISION-MAKING BODY	NUMBER OF WOMEN			PER CENT WOMEN			TOTAL NUMBER OF MEMBERS*		
	1966/67	1976/77	1986/87	1966/67	1976/77	1986/87	1966/67	1976/77	1986/87
The Parliament as a whole (Riksdag)									
Advisory Council on Foreign Affairs	2	1	2	13%	8%	17%	16	12	12
War Delegation									
Su. Del. to the Nordic Council	1	6	9	6%	33%	45%	16	18	20
Executive Committee of the Riksdag									
Interparliamentary Group	1	1	4	17%	14%	57%	6	7	7
Standing Committee on Defence	0	3	3	0%	10%	32%	12	16	19
Standing Comm. on Foreign Affairs	2	2	7	13%	13%	33%	16	16	21
ALL DECISION-MAKING BODIES	6	13	28	9%	19%	35%	66	69	79
THE RIKSDAG NOT INCLUDED	6	13	28	9%	19%	35%	66	69	79

* Both men and women.

(A) DECISION-MAKING BODIES DEALING WITH ALL THREE ISSUES. / (A1) THE SWEDISH PARLIAMENT (THE RIKSDAG).

(A1.1) THE SWEDISH PARLIAMENT, TOTAL BY YEAR AND SEX. (Riksdagen)

| | 1966/67 | | | 1976/77 | 1986/87 |
	1st Chamber	2nd Chamber	Total	Total	Total
WOMEN	16	34	50	80	113
MEN	135	199	334	269	236
TOTAL	151	233	384	349	349
% OF TOTAL					
WOMEN	10.6%	14.6%	13.0%	22.9%	32.4%
MEN	89.4%	85.4%	87.0%	77.1%	67.6%

Source: Riksdagsmatrikel 1967, Part I, page 30 and
Part II, page 43. (Jan 1967)
Riksdagsmatrikel 1976/77, Part I Page 78. (Nov 1976)
Sveriges Riksdag 1986/87, page 8. (Nov 1986)

The Swedish Parliament changed from two to one Chamber in 1971. Before 1971 the Parliamentary session = calender year. Since 1971 the Parliamentary session = October - May. To get the best comparison the figures for the decision-making bodies within the Parliament are taken from January 1967, November 1976 and November 1986.

Before 1971, when the Parliament had two Chambers, it was one Speaker of Parliament and two Deputy Speakers in each Chamber. Since 1971 there is one Speaker of Parliament and three Deputy Speakers.

The Speaker of Parliament has always been a man. In 1986/87 one of the three Deputy Speakers (the First Deputy Speaker) was a women. In 1966/67 and 1976/77 all Deputy Speakers were Men.

(A1.2) THE ADVISORY COUNCIL ON FOREIGN AFFAIRS (Utrikesnämnden).

(A1.2a) Total by year and sex.

	1966/67	1976/77	1986/87
WOMEN	3	3	4
MEN	30	17	19
TOTAL	33	20	23
% OF TOTAL			
WOMEN	9.1%	15.0%	17.4%
MEN	90.9%	85.0%	82.6%

Source: Riksdagsmatrikel 1967, Part III, page 1. (Jan 1967)
Riksdagsmatrikel 1976/77, Part II, page 49. (Nov 1976)
Sveriges Riksdag 1986/87, page 112. (Nov 1986)

The Advisory Council on Foreign Affairs was established in 1921. Since 1971 the Council consists of the Head of State (the King, who is the Chairperson), the Speaker of Parliament and 9 permanent members. The Council has at least 12 deputy members, including the three Deputy Speakers. (Source: "Norstedts uppslagsbok", page 1372, and the Riksdag Act (Riksdagsordningen), chapter 8, paragraph 7.)

In table A1.2b the Chairperson, the King, is included in permanent members.

(A1.2b) Positions of members, by year and sex.

(A1.2ba) 1966/67.

	Permanent	Deputy	Total
WOMEN	1	2	3
MEN	16	14	30
TOTAL	17	16	33
% OF TOTAL			
WOMEN	5.9%	12.5%	9.1%
MEN	94.1%	87.5%	90.9%

Source: Riksdagsmatrikel 1967, Part III, page 1. (Jan 1967)

Before 1971 the permanent and deputy members of the Standing Committee on Foreign Affairs were chosen also as members of the Advisory Council on Foreign Affairs.

(A1.2bb) 1976/77.

	Permanent	Deputy	Total
WOMEN	2	1	3
MEN	9	11	20
TOTAL	11	12	23
% OF TOTAL			
WOMEN	18.2%	3.3%	13.0%
MEN	81.8%	91.7%	87.0%

Source: Riksdagsmatrikel 1976/77, Part II, page 49. (Nov 1976)

(A1.2bc) 1986/87.

	Permanent	Deputy	Total
WOMEN	2	2	4
MEN	9	10	19
TOTAL	11	12	23
% OF TOTAL			
WOMEN	18.2%	16.7%	17.4%
MEN	81.8%	83.3%	82.6%

Source: Sveriges Riksdag 1986/87, page 112. (Nov 1986)

(A) DECISION-MAKING BODIES DEALING WITH ALL THREE ISSUES. / (A1) THE SWEDISH PARLIAMENT (THE RIKSDAG).

(A1.3) THE WAR DELEGATION (Krigsdelegationen)

Permanent members by year and sex.

	1st Chamb. 1966/67	2nd Chamb.	Total	1976/77 Total	1986/87 Total
WOMEN	2	4	6	6	9
MEN	24	21	45	45	42
TOTAL	26	25	51	51	51
% OF TOTAL					
WOMEN	7.7%	16.0%	11.8%	11.8%	17.6%
MEN	92.3%	84.0%	88.2%	88.2%	82.4%

Source: Riksdagens Årsbok 1967, sid 63 and 71. (Jan 1967)
Riksdagen 1976/77 Register/Personregister,
Page 5-71. (Nov 1976)
Sveriges Riksdag 1986/87, page 113. (Nov 1986)

The establishment of a War Delegation was included in the
constitution in 1964/65. The War Delegation is a Parliament in
miniature, proportionally composed of the political parties in the
Parliament. The War Delegation consists of 50 permanent members and
the Speaker of Parliament, who is the Chairperson. The War Delegation
takes over duties of the Riksdag if it is impossible for the Riksdag
to meet normally in case of war.
(Source: Halvarsson, "Sveriges Statsskick. En faktasamling", page 11.)

(A1.4) THE SWEDISH DELEGATION TO THE NORDIC COUNCIL (Nordiska Rådets svenska delegation)

(A1.4a) Total by year and sex.

	1966/67	1976/77	1986/87
WOMEN	4	9	16
MEN	28	27	24
TOTAL	32	36	40
% OF TOTAL			
WOMEN	12.5%	25.0%	40.0%
MEN	87.5%	75.0%	60.0%

Source: Riksdagsmatrikel 1967, Part III, page 60. (Jan 1967)
Riksdagsmatrikel 1976/77, Part II, page 71-73. (Nov 1976)
Sveriges Riksdag 1986/87, page 116. (Nov 1986)

Permanent members (incl. Chairperson and Deputy Chairperson) and deputy
members are included in the tables A1.4a and A1.4b. The table
A1.4b shows also the sex of the Administrative Director (Kanslichef) of
the Committee (not included in "TOTAL").

(A1.4b) Positions of members, by year and sex.

(A1.4ba) 1966/67.

	Permanent Total	Chairp.	Dep.Chairp.	Deputy	TOTAL	Adm. Dir.
WOMEN	3			1	4	
MEN	13			15	28	M
TOTAL	16			16	32	M
% OF TOTAL						
WOMEN	18.8%			6.3%	12.5%	
MEN	81.3%			93.8%	87.5%	

Source: Riksdagsmatrikel 1967, Part III, page 60. (Jan 1967)

(A1.4bb) 1976/77.

	Permanent Total	Chairp.	Dep.Chairp.	Deputy	TOTAL	Adm. Dir.
WOMEN	3			6	9	
MEN	15			12	27	M
TOTAL	18			18	36	M
% OF TOTAL						
WOMEN	16.7%			33.3%	25.0%	
MEN	83.3%			66.7%	75.0%	

Source: Riksdagsmatrikel 1976/77, Part II, page 71-73. (Nov 1976)

(A1.4bc) 1986/87.

	Permanent Total	Chairp.	Dep.Chairp.	Deputy	TOTAL	Adm. Dir.
WOMEN	7			9	16	
MEN	13			11	24	M
TOTAL	20			20	40	M
% OF TOTAL						
WOMEN	35.0%			45.0%	40.0%	
MEN	65.0%			55.0%	60.0%	

Source: Sveriges Riksdag 1986/87, page 116. (Nov 1986)

(A) DECISION-MAKING BODIES DEALING WITH ALL THREE ISSUES.

(A1.5) THE EXECUTIVE COMMITTEE OF THE RIKSDAG INTERPARLIAMENTARY GROUP (Styrelsen för Riksdagens interparlamentariska grupp)

(A1.5a) Total by year and sex.

	1966/67	1976/77	1986/87
WOMEN	2	6	6
MEN	13	10	10
TOTAL	15	16	16
% OF TOTAL			
WOMEN	13.3%	37.5%	37.5%
MEN	86.7%	62.5%	62.5%

Source: Riksdagsmatrikel 1967, Part III, page 64. (Jan 1967)
Riksdagsmatrikel 1976/77, Part II, Page 75. (Nov 1976)
Sveriges Riksdag 1986/87, page 118. (Nov 1986)

Permanent members (incl. Chairperson and Deputy Chairperson) and deputy members are included in tables A1.5a and A1.5b.

(A1.5b) Positions of members, by year and sex.

(A1.5ba) 1966/67.

	Total	Permanent Chairp.	Dep.Chairp.	Deputy	TOTAL
WOMEN	1			1	2
MEN	8	M	3	5	13
TOTAL	9			6	15
% OF TOTAL					
WOMEN	11.1%				13.3%
MEN	88.9%				86.7%

Source: Riksdagsmatrikel 1967, Part III, page 64. (Jan 1967)

(A1.5bb) 1976/77.

	Total	Permanent Chairp.	Dep.Chairp.	Deputy	TOTAL
WOMEN	5		M	1	6
MEN	4	M		6	10
TOTAL	9			7	16
% OF TOTAL					
WOMEN	55.6%				37.5%
MEN	44.4%				62.5%

Source: Riksdagsmatrikel 1976/77, Part II, page 75. (Nov 1976)

(A1.5bc) 1986/87.

	Total	Permanent Chairp.	Dep.Chairp.	Deputy	TOTAL
WOMEN	2		M	4	6
MEN	7	M		3	10
TOTAL	9			7	16
% OF TOTAL					
WOMEN	22.2%				37.5%
MEN	77.8%				62.5%

Source: Sveriges Riksdag 1986/87, page 118. (Nov 1986)

(B) DECISION-MAKING BODIES DEALING WITH DEFENCE ISSUES.

(B1) THE SWEDISH PARLIAMENT (THE RIKSDAG).

(B1.1) (PARLIAMENTARY) STANDING COMMITTEE ON DEFENCE (Försvarsutskottet)

(B1.1a) Total by year and sex.

	1966/67	1976/77	1986/87
WOMEN	(1)	5	9
MEN	(17)	26	25
TOTAL	(18)	31	34
% OF TOTAL			
WOMEN	5.6%	16.1%	26.5%
MEN	94.4%	83.9%	73.5%

Source: Riksdagsmatrikel 1967, Part III, page 9-10, 15. (Jan 1967)
Riksdagsmatrikel 1976/77, Part II, Page 19-20. (Nov 1976)
Sveriges Riksdag 1986/87, page 100. (Nov 1986)

The Standing Committee on Defence did not exist in 1966/67. The figures for 1966/67 shows the members of the Standing Committee of Supply/ 1st Division (Statsutsk.: 1:a Avd.), who were responsible for, among other things, the expenses of the Ministry of Defence (including expenses for the Armed Forces and the Civil Defence).

The figures for 1976/77 and 1986/87 are accordingly not fully comparable with the figures for 1966/67, which shows the members of the Standing Committee on Defence.

Permanent members (incl. Chairperson and Deputy Chairperson; for 1966/67 Chairperson and Deputy Chairperson of St. Comm. of Supply/1st Div.) and deputy members are included in tables B1.1a and B1.1b. Table B1.1b shows also the sex of the Secretary (Kanslichef) of the Committee (not included in "TOTAL").

(B1.1b) Position of members, by year and sex.

(B1.1ba) 1966/67. Standing Committee of Supply/1st Division

	Total	Permanent Chairp.	Dep.Chairp.	Deputy	TOTAL	Secr.
WOMEN	1			0	1	
MEN	5	M		12	17	M
TOTAL	6			12	18	
% OF TOTAL						
WOMEN	16.7%			0.0%	5.6%	
MEN	83.3%			100.0%	94.4%	

Source: Riksdagsmatrikel 1966/67, Part III, page 9-10 and 15. (Jan 1967)

(B1.1bb) 1976/77.

	Total	Permanent Chairp.	Dep.Chairp.	Deputy	TOTAL	Secr.
WOMEN	2		M	3	5	
MEN	13	M		13	26	M
TOTAL	15			16	31	
% OF TOTAL						
WOMEN	13.3%			18.8%	16.1%	
MEN	86.7%			81.3%	83.9%	

Source: Riksdagsmatrikel 1976/77, Part II, page 19-20. (Nov 1976)

(B) DECISION-MAKING BODIES DEALING WITH DEFENCE ISSUES.

(B1.1bb) 1986/87.

	Total		Permanent Chairp.		Dep.Chairp.		Deputy		TOTAL		Secr.
	W	M	W	M	W	M	W	M	W	M		M
WOMEN	3						6		9			
MEN	12							13		25		
TOTAL	15						19		34			
% OF TOTAL WOMEN	20.0%						31.6%		26.5%			
MEN	80.0%							68.4%		73.5%		

Source: Sveriges Riksdag 1986/87, page 100. (Nov 1986)

(C) DECISION-MAKING BODIES DEALING WITH DISARMAMENT ISSUES.

(C1) THE SWEDISH PARLIAMENT (THE RIKSDAG).

Non

(D) DECISION-MAKING BODIES DEALING WITH FOREIGN AFFAIRS AND FOREIGN AID.

(D1) THE SWEDISH PARLIAMENT (THE RIKSDAG).

(D1.1) (PARLIAMENTARY) STANDING COMMITTEE ON FOREIGN AFFAIRS (Utrikesutskottet).

(D1.1a) Total by year and sex.

	1966/67	1976/77	1986/87
WOMEN	3	7	12
MEN	29	24	24
TOTAL	32	31	36
% OF TOTAL WOMEN	9.4%	22.6%	33.3%
MEN	90.6%	77.4%	66.7%

Source: Riksdagsmatrikel 1967, Part III, page 1-3. (Jan 1967)
Riksdagsmatrikel 1976/77, Part II, page 16-17. (Nov 1976)
Sveriges Riksdag 1986/87, page 99. (Nov 1986)

Until 1971 the same people were chosen as members in both the Advisory Council on Foreign Affairs and the Standing Committee on Foreign Affairs, with the exception of the Head of the State, who was (and is) the Chairperson of the Advisory Council on Foreign Affairs. The Standing Committee is the preparing body of the Parliament in issues of Foreign Affairs.

Permanent members (incl. Chairperson and Deputy Chairperson) and deputy members are included in tables D1.1a and D1.1b. Table D1.1b shows also the sex of the Secretary (Kanslichef) of the Committee, (not included in "TOTAL").

(D) DECISION-MAKING BODIES DEALING WITH FOREIGN AFFAIRS AND FOREIGN AID.

(D1.1b) Positions of members, by year and sex.

(D1.1ba) 1966/67.

	Total		Permanent Chairp.		Dep.Chairp.		Deputy		TOTAL		Secr.
	W	M	W	M	W	M	W	M	W	M		M
WOMEN	1						2		3			
MEN	15							14		29		32
TOTAL	16						16		32			
% OF TOTAL WOMEN	6.3%						12.5%		9.4%			
MEN	93.9%							87.5%		90.6%		

Source: Riksdagsmatrikel 1967, Part III, page 1-3. (Jan 1967)

(D1.1bb) 1976/77.

	Total		Permanent Chairp.		Dep.Chairp.		Deputy		TOTAL		Secr.
	W	M	W	M	W	M	W	M	W	M		M
WOMEN	5						2		7			
MEN	10							14		24		31
TOTAL	15						16		31			
% OF TOTAL WOMEN	33.3%						12.5%		22.6%			
MEN	66.7%							87.5%		77.4%		

Source: Riksdagsmatrikel 1976/77, Part II, page 16-17. (Nov 1976)

(D1.1bc) 1986/87.

	Total		Permanent Chairp.		Dep.Chairp.		Deputy		TOTAL		Secr.
	W	M	W	M	W	M	W	M	W	M		M
WOMEN	5						7		12			
MEN	10							14		24		36
TOTAL	15						21		36			
% OF TOTAL WOMEN	33.3%						33.3%		33.3%			
MEN	66.7%							66.7%		66.7%		

Source: Sveriges Riksdag 1986/87, page 99. (Nov 1986)

Appendix 2

Statistical Data of the Representation of Women in Decision-Making Bodies within the Swedish Government and the Government Office.

Information - Tables in Appendix 2A:

In tables A2.2, B2.1 and D2.1 the included persons are categorized, after their titles, into three categories:
Head Officials ("Heads")
Advisers and
Officials responsible for processing issues ("Proc").

The titles changes, however, over time and it has in some cases been difficult to categorize the person after his/her title. I have therefore chosen to list, below each table, the titles (persons) included in each category.

Appendix 2A

The Government and the Government Office

Table 1: Statistical Figures over Equal Representation within the Government Office (the Office of
the Prime Minister and the Ministries).

Table 1a: Statistical Figures over Equal Representation within the Government Office (not including
Ministry for Foreign Affairs). July 1986.

Category of Salery[1]	Per Cent Women	Number of Women	Total Number
Head off.[2]	12	22	177
N 24 - N 27	26	36	136
N 23 - N 24	43	60	139
N 13 - N 22	54	130	242
N 8 - N 16	86	74	86
N 6 - N 14	91	364	402
Bg1C/N4 - N 9	71	277	391
All	61	963	1.573

Table 1b: Statistical Figures over Equal Representation within the
Ministry for Foreign Affairs. October 1986.

Category of Salery[1]	Per Cent Women	Number of Women	Total Number
Head off.[2]	5	8	168
N 24 - N 27	6	10	158
N 23 - N 24	25	42	165
N 12 - N 22	47	113	241
N 8 - N 16	82	67	82
N 6 - N 14	87	161	186
N 6 -·N 14	43	3	7
N 4 - N 14	94	287	306
Bg 1C/N 4 - N 9	71	164	230
BI	72	13	18
HL	31	5	16
All	55	873	1577

[1] Employees with a salary down to category N 13 are in most cases officials responsible for processing
an issue or matter (handläggare). Also in lower categories there can be officials responsible for
processing issues, but not as many as in higher categories.

[2] The salery category "Head officials" include, according to the source: Head officials (for example
Under-Secretaries for Legal Affairs (rättschef) and Permanent Under-Secretaries (expeditionschef),
Assistant Under-Secretaries (dep.råd) and some Special Advisers (sakkunniga). It does not include,
Cabinet Ministers (statsråd), Under-Secretarties of State (statssekr.), Legal and Political Advisers
(rättssakkunniga, politiskt sakkunniga). Special Advisers are not included in any other categories
then the category "head officials".

Source: Central Services Office for the Ministries, "Handlingsprogram för jämställdhet i
regeringskansliet", page 3, 4 and 9.

Table 1c: Per Cent and Number of Women by Ministry[1] and Category of Salery. July and October 1986[2].
The Ministries Ranked after Female Representation.

Head Officials:

Ministry[1]	Per Cent Women	Number of Women	Total Number
SB	40	2	5
Bo	27	3	11
S	25	4	16
A	14	2	14
Ju	13	2	16
U	13	2	16
Jo	10	1	10
K	10	1	10
Fi	9	3	32
C	7	1	15
UD	5	8	168[3]
I	5	1	19
Fö	0	0	12
FK	0	0	1

Salery Category N 24 - N 27:

Ministry[1]	Per Cent Women	Number of Women	Total Number
U	71	10	14
FK	50	2	4
Ju	43	3	7
S	36	4	7
A	33	2	6
C	31	4	9
Fi	26	5	19
Jo	25	2	8
Fö	15	2	13
I	9	2	22
UD	6	10	158[3]
SB	0	0	1
Bo	0	0	8
K	0	0	10

Salery Category N 23 -N 24:

Ministry[1]	Per Cent Women	Number of Women	Total Number
Ju	100	3	3
U	64	16	25
A	54	7	13
Bo	50	5	10
FK	50	4	8
Fi	47	7	15
S	47	7	15
C	30	3	10

(continued next page)

Salery Category N 23 -N 24: (continued)

Ministry[1]	Per Cent Women	Number of Women	Total Number
I	29	7	24
UD	25	42	165[3]
Fö	17	1	6
K	0	0	4
Jo	0	0	6

Salery Category N 13 - N 22:

Ministry[1]	Per Cent Women	Number of Women	Total Number
SB	100	1	1
A	67	26	39
C	67	6	9
K	67	6	9
U	65	24	37
I	59	16	27
FK	50	6	12
Jo	50	9	18
UD	47	113	241[3]
Fö	43	9	21
Ju	43	3	7
S	39	7	18
Fi	39	12	31
Bo	38	5	13

[1] Abbreviations: See below.

[2] The figures over the Ministry for Foreign Affairs from October 1986, all other figures from July 1986.

[3] The Ministry for Foreign Affairs has different Salery Categories than the other ministries and are accordingly not fully comparable with them. See table 1b.

Source: Central Services Office for the Ministries, "Handlingsprogram för jämställdhet i regeringskansliet", page 5-6 and 9.

Abbreviations used in table 1c:

A = Ministry of Labour (Arbetsmarknadsdepartementet)
Bo = Ministry of Housing and Physical Planning (Bostadsdep.)
C = Ministry of Public Administration (Civildep.)
Fi = Ministry of Finance (Finansdep.)
FK = Central Services Office for the Ministries (Regeringskansliets Förvaltningskontor).
Fö = Ministry of Defence (Försvarsdep.)
I = Ministry of Industry (Industridep.)
Jo = Ministry of Agriculture (Jordbruksdep.)
Ju = Ministry of Justice (Justitiedep.)
K = Ministry of Transport and Communications (Kommunikationsdepartementet)
S = Ministry of Health and Social Affairs (Socialdep.)
SB = Office of the Prime Minister (Statrådsberedningen)
U = Ministry of Education and Cultural Affairs (Utbildningsdepartementet)
UD = Ministry for Foreign Affairs (Utrikesdep.)

SUMMARY OF DECISION-MAKING BODIES - THE GOVERNMENT.

TABLE 2: Number of and Per Cent Women, All Officials, by Year.

NAME OF DECISION-MAKING BODY	NUMBER OF WOMEN 1966/67	1976/77	1986/87	PER CENT WOMEN 1966/67	1976/77	1986/87	TOTAL NUMBER OF MEMBERS** 1966/67	1976/77	1986/87	No of table
The Government as a whole	2	5	5	11.8%	25.0%	25.0%	17	20	20	(A2.1)
Office of the Prime Minister	0	5	13	0.0%	26.3%	40.6%	6	19	32	(A2.2)
Ministry of Defence	1	6	13	2.3%	8.8%	16.3%	43	68	80	(B2.1)
Ministry for Foreign Affairs	3	15	108	3.8%	10.7%	32.7%	78	140	330	(D2.1)
ALL DECISION-MAKING BODIES	6	31	139	4.2%	12.6%	30.1%	144	247	462	
THE GOVERNMENT NOT INCLUDED	4	26	134	3.1%	11.5%	30.3%	127	227	442	

* See the following tables in App. 2A for detailed information.
** Both men and women.

TABLE 3: Number of and Per Cent Women, Head Officials, by Year.

NAME OF DECISION-MAKING BODY	NUMBER OF WOMEN 1966/67	1976/77	1986/87	PER CENT WOMEN 1966/67	1976/77	1986/87	TOTAL NUMBER OF MEMBERS* 1966/67	1976/77	1986/87
The Government as a whole	2	5	5	11.8%	25.0%	25.0%	17	20	20
Office of the Prime Minister	0	0	2	0.0%	0.0%	28.6%	3	4	7
Ministry of Defence	0	0	0	0.0%	12.5%	0.0%	18	16	20
Ministry for Foreign Affairs	1	2	10	2.8%	4.7%	10.1%	36	43	99
ALL DECISION-MAKING BODIES	3	9	17	4.1%	10.8%	11.6%	74	83	146
THE GOVERNMENT NOT INCLUDED	1	4	12	1.8%	6.3%	9.5%	57	63	126

* Both men and women

(A) DECISION-MAKING BODIES DEALING WITH ALL THREE ISSUES. / (A2) THE SWEDISH GOVERNMENT.

(A2.1) THE SWEDISH GOVERNMENT, TOTAL BY YEAR AND SEX.

	1966/67	1976/77	1986/87
WOMEN	2	5	5
MEN	15	15	15
TOTAL	17	20	20
% OF TOTAL			
WOMEN	11.8%	25.0%	25.0%
MEN	88.2%	75.0%	75.0%

Source: Sveriges Statskalender 1967, page 57. (Jan 67)
Sveriges Statskalender 1977, page 43. (Jan 77)
Sveriges Statskalender 1986, page 55. (Jan 86)

(A2.2) THE OFFICE OF THE PRIME MINISTER. (Statsrådsberedningen)

(A2.2a) Total by year and sex.

	1966/67	1976/77	1986/87
WOMEN	0	5	13
MEN	6	14	19
TOTAL	6	19	32
% OF TOTAL			
WOMEN	0.0%	26.3%	40.6%
MEN	100.0%	73.7%	59.4%

Source: Sveriges Statskalender 1967, page 59. (Jan 67)
Sveriges Statskalender 1977, page 44. (Jan 77)
Sveriges Statskalender 1986, page 57. (Jan 86)

In tables A2.2a and A2.2b the following are included:
Head officials ("Heads")
Advisers ("Advisers")
Officials responsible for processing issues ("Proc.")

The following officials are included in Head Officials (chefs-tjänstemän): The Prime Minister (premiärministern), Under-Secretary of State (statssekreterare), Under-Secretary for Legal Affairs (rättschef), Director of Policy Planning (planeringschef), Assistant Under-Secretaries (departementsråd) and Deputy Assistant Under-Secretaries (kansliråd).

The following are included in Advisers (sakkunniga): Political, Legal and Special Advisers (politiska, juridiska och övriga sakkunniga).

The following are included in the officials responsible for processing issues (beredande, handläggande personal): Press Officer (press-sekreterare), Principal and Senior Administrative Officers (departementssekreterare). In the source "Sveriges Statskalender 1986" are some persons categorized as "other officials". These persons are here included as Officials responsible for processing issues.

No consideration has been taken to leave of absence.

(A2.2b) Positions of members, by year and sex.

(A2.2ba) 1966/67.

	Heads	Advisers	Proc.	Total
WOMEN	0	-	0	0
MEN	3	-	3	6
TOTAL	3	-	3	6
% OF TOTAL				
WOMEN	0.0%	-	0.0%	0.0%
MEN	100.0%	-	100.0%	100.0%

Source: Sveriges Statskalender 1967, page 59.

(A2.2bb) 1976/77.

	Heads	Advisers	Proc.	Total
WOMEN	0	4	1	5
MEN	4	9	1	14
TOTAL	4	13	2	19
% OF TOTAL				
WOMEN	0.0%	30.8%	50.0%	26.3%
MEN	100.0%	69.2%	50.0%	73.7%

Source: Sveriges Statskalender 1977, page 44.

(A2.2bc) 1986/87.

	Heads	Advisers	Proc.	Total
WOMEN	2	7	4	13
MEN	5	7	7	19
TOTAL	7	14	11	32
% OF TOTAL				
WOMEN	28.6%	50.0%	36.4%	40.6%
MEN	71.4%	50.0%	63.6%	59.4%

Source: Sveriges Statskalender 1986, page 57.

(B) DECISION-MAKING BODIES DEALING WITH DEFENCE ISSUES.   (B2) THE SWEDISH GOVERNMENT.

(B2.1) THE MINISTRY OF DEFENCE (Försvarsdepartementet).

(B2.1a) Total by year and sex.

	1966/67	1976/77	1986/87
WOMEN	1	6	13
MEN	42	62	67
TOTAL	43	68	80
% OF TOTAL			
WOMEN	2.3%	8.8%	16.3%
MEN	97.7%	91.2%	83.8%

Source: Sveriges Statskalender 1967, page 65-66. (Jan 67)
        Sveriges Statskalender 1977, page 51-52. (Jan 77)
        Sveriges Statskalender 1986, page 64-66. (Jan 86)

In tables B2.1a and B2.1b the following are included:
Head officials ("Heads")
Advisers ("Advisers")
Officials responsible for processing issues ("Proc.")

The following officials are included in Head Officials (chefs-
tjänstemän): The Cabinet Minister (statsråd), Under-Secretary
of State (statssekreterare), Under-Secretary for Legal Affairs
(rättschef), Permanent Under-Secretary (expeditionschef), Assistant Under-Secretaries (departementsråd), Deputy Assistant Under-
Secretaries (kansliråd), Major-General (gen.major), Colonel
(överste) and Adv., National Security Affairs (överingenjör).

The following are inlcuded in Advisers (sakkunniga): Political,
Legal and Special Advisers (politisk, juridisk och övriga sakkunniga).

The following are included in the officials responsible for processing
issues (beredande, handläggande, personal): Information Officer (inf.-
sekr.) Principal and Senior Administrative Officers (Departementssekreterare, avdelningsdir.), Lieutnant-Colonel (överstelöjtnant),
Major (major), Commander (kommendörkapten), Lietnant-Commander (örlogs-
kapten), Associate Judge of Appeal (hovrättsassesor), and First
Researcher (förste forskare).

No consideration has been taken to leave of absence.

(B2.1b) Positions of members, by year and sex.

(B2.1ba) 1966/67.

	Heads	Advisers	Proc.	Total
WOMEN	0	0	1	1
MEN	18	6	18	42
TOTAL	18	6	19	43
% OF TOTAL				
WOMEN	0.0%	0.0%	5.3%	2.3%
MEN	100.0%	100.0%	94.7%	97.7%

Source: Sveriges Statskalender 1967, page 65-66. (Jan 67)

(B2.1bb) 1976/77.

	Heads	Advisers	Proc.	Total	
WOMEN	2	1	3	6	Both women in
MEN	14	19	29	62	"Heads": Deputy
TOTAL	16	20	32	68	Assistant Under-
% OF TOTAL					Secretaries.
WOMEN	12.5%	5.0%	9.4%	8.8%	
MEN	87.5%	95.0%	90.6%	91.2%	

Source: Sveriges Statskalender 1977, page 51-52. (Jan 77)

(B2.1bc) 1986/87.

	Heads	Advisers	Proc.	Total
WOMEN	0	1	12	13
MEN	20	9	38	67
TOTAL	20	10	50	80
% OF TOTAL				
WOMEN	0.0%	10.0%	24.0%	16.3%
MEN	100.0%	90.0%	76.0%	83.8%

Source: Sveriges Statskalender 1986, page 64-66. (Jan 86)

(C) DECISION-MAKING BODIES DEALING WITH DISARMAMENT ISSUES.

(C2) THE SWEDISH GOVERNMENT.

Non

(D) DECISION-MAKING BODIES DEALING WITH ISSUES CONCERNING FOREIGN AFFAIRS AND FOREIGN AID.

(D2) THE SWEDISH GOVERNMENT.

(D2.1) THE MINISTRY FOR FOREIGN AFFAIRS (Utrikesdepartementet)

(D2.1a) Total by year and sex.

	1966/67	1976/77	1986/87
WOMEN	3	15	108
MEN	75	125	222
TOTAL	78	140	330
% OF TOTAL			
WOMEN	3.8%	10.7%	32.7%
MEN	96.2%	89.3%	67.3%

Source: Sveriges Statskalender 1967, page 62-65. (Jan 67)
Sveriges Statskalender 1977, page 46-49. (Jan 77)
Sveriges Statskalender 1986, page 58-64. (Jan 86)

In tables D2.1a and D2.1b the following are included:
Head officials ("Heads")
Advisers ("Advisers")
Officials responsible for processing issues ("Proc.")

The following officials are included in Head Officials (Chefs-tjänsteman): The Cabinet Minister (statsråd), Under-Secretaries of State (statssekreterare), Under-Secretary for Legal Affairs (rättschef), Permanent Under-Secretary (expeditionschef), Under-Secretary of State for Foreign Affairs (kabinettsekreterare), Minister (minister i utrikesförvaltningen), Ambassadors (ambassadörer), Inspector-General, Foreign Affairs (utrikesförvaltningens inspektör), Counsellors (ambassadråd), Assistant-Under Secretaries (departementsråd, samt utbildningschef), Deputy Assistant Under-Secretaries (kansliråd) and Administrative Director (kanslichef).

The following are included in Advisers (sakkunniga): Political, Legal and Special Advisers (politiska, juridiska och övriga sakkunniga).

The following are included in the officials responsible for processing issues (beredande, handläggande, personal): Information Officer (inf. sekr.) and Senior Administrative Officers (departementssekreterare).

No consideration has been taken to leave of absence.

(D2.1b) Positions of members, by year and sex.

(D2.1ba) 1966/67.

	Heads	Advisers	Proc.	Total
WOMEN	1	0	2	3
MEN	35	2	38	75
TOTAL	36	2	40	78
% OF TOTAL				
WOMEN	2.8%	0.0%	5.0%	3.8%
MEN	97.2%	100.0%	95.0%	96.2%

Source: Sveriges Statskalender 1967, page 62-65. (Jan 67)

(D2.1bb) 1976/77.

	Heads	Advisers	Proc.	Total
WOMEN	2	0	13	15
MEN	41	9	75	125
TOTAL	43	9	88	140
% OF TOTAL				
WOMEN	4.7%	0.0%	14.8%	10.7%
MEN	95.3%	100.0%	85.2%	89.3%

Source: Sveriges Statskalender 1976, page 46-49. (Jan 77)

One of the two women included in "Heads" was a Cabinet Minister and Head of the Ministry for Foreign Affairs.

(D2.1bc) 1986/87.

	Heads	Advisers	Proc.	Total
WOMEN	10	2	96	108
MEN	89	9	124	222
TOTAL	99	11	220	330
% OF TOTAL				
WOMEN	10.1%	18.2%	43.6%	32.7%
MEN	89.9%	81.8%	56.4%	67.3%

Source: Sveriges Statskalender 1986, page 58-64. (Jan 86)

Appendix 2B

The Ministerial Committees

Information - Tables in Appendix 2B.

Appendix 2B include: table 1-2 (ministerial committees subordinated to all ministries), 3-4 (summary tables over the 39 ministerial committees included in this study) and one table for each of the 39 ministerial committees. 23 of these 39 committees are subordinated to the Ministry of Defence (tables B2.2.1-23), and 16 subordinated to the Ministry for Foreign Affairs (tables D2.2.1-14 as well as tables C3.1 and D3.1 in Appendix 3A).

These 39 tables show, for each of the 39 ministerial committees, the total number of members, by position and sex. Each committee has permanent members (including Chairperson and Deputy Chairperson) and a secretariate, and could also include Special Advisers and/or Experts.

Each of these 39 ministerial committees worked during a shorter period of time (one to six years) within the period 1966 - 1987 (one started 1961). The committees are listed after the date when the committee's work ended, with the last committee first. As the committees work lasted over a period of time, they are mapped out at two occasions: when the committee started its work and when it ended it, that is, "Start" and "End" in the tables below.

The 39 ministerial committees included below are committees with political importance and/or of special interest for this study. The total number of ministerial committees set up by Ministry of Defence during the period 1966 - 1987 was 103. The corresponding figure for the Ministry for Foreign Affairs was 41.

The source is the "Kommittéberättelsen" (Committee Report; before 1975: "Riksdagsberättelsen" - Riksdag Report) in which the Government report, every year, to Parliament (the Riksdag) the committees which are working during the year. The Committee Report is compiled by the Ministry of Justice.

TABLE 1. CHAIRPERSONS IN MINISTERIAL COMMITTEES SUBORDINATED TO ALL MINISTRIES, 1986.
Ranked after Female Participation.

MINISTRY	NUMBER OF		PER CENT	
	WOMEN	MEN	WOMEN	MEN
Ministry of Labour	4	10	29	71
Ministry of Health & Social Affairs	6	19	24	76
Ministry for Foreign Affairs	2	7	22	78
Ministry of Defence	2	14	12	88
Ministry of Transport & Communications	1	8	11	89
Ministry of Educations & Cultural Aff.	2	24	8	92
Ministry of Finance	4	38	0	100
Ministry of Housing & Physical Planning	-	7	-	100
Ministry of Agriculture	-	15	-	100
Ministry of Industry	-	20	-	100
Ministry of Public Administration	-	21	-	100
Ministry of Justice	-	40	-	100
TOTAL NUMBER	18	221 *	8	92

* According to the source, the total number in this column is 219.

Source: Statistics Sweden (SCB), "Kvinno- och Mansvär(l)den", page 173.

TABLE 2. PERMANENT MEMBERS (NOT INCL. CHAIRPERSONS) IN MINISTERIAL COMMITTEES SUBORDINATED TO ALL MINISTRIES, 1986.
Ranked after Female Participation.

MINISTRY	NUMBER OF		PER CENT	
	WOMEN	MEN	WOMEN	MEN
Ministry of Health & Social Affairs	29	36	45	55
Ministry of Agriculture	11	29	28	72
Ministry of Educations & Cultural Aff.	13	43	23	77
Ministry of Public Administration	21	80	21	79
Ministry of Housing & Physical Planning	4	17	19	81
Ministry of Justice	27	124	18	82
Ministry of Labour	7	31	18	82
Ministry of Finance	24	122	16	84
Ministry of Defence	8	50	14	86
Ministry for Foreign Affairs	8	24	14	86
Ministry of Industry	4	49	8	92
Ministry of Transport & Communications	1	12	8	92
TOTAL NUMBER	153	617	20	80

Source: Statistics Sweden (SCB), "Kvinno- och Mansvär(l)den", page 173.

TABLE 3: SUMMARY OF ALL MINISTERIAL COMMITTEES, ALL MEMBERS* BY SEX.

NAME OF COMMITTEE	TOTAL NUMBER OF MEMBERS Start	End**	OF WHICH: WOMEN Start	End	MEN Start	End	PERCENT WOMEN OF TOTAL Start	End	No of table

Table 3a: MINISTERIAL COMMITTEES SUBORDINATED TO THE MINISTRY OF DEFENCE:

NAME OF COMMITTEE	Start	End	Women Start	Women End	Men Start	Men End	%W Start	%W End	No of table
1984 Parl. Comm. on Defence Policy	18	22	1	2	17	20	5.6%	9.1%	(B2.2.1)
Comm. on the Supreme Oper. Command	7	7	1	1	6	6	14.3%	14.3%	(B2.2.2)
Expert Study on Resistance Questios	8	8	2	2	6	6	25.0%	25.0%	(B2.2.3)
Su. Internat. Humanitarian Law Comm.	17	20	0	1	17	19	0.0%	5.0%	(B2.2.4)
Submarine Defence Committee	8	8	1	1	7	7	12.5%	12.5%	(B2.2.5)
Comm. on Oper. Command of the Total Defence Org. in the Cabinet and Min.	2	2	0	0	2	2	0.0%	0.0%	(B2.2.6)
Comm. for Planning & Inf. for Psyc. Def.	10	11	1	2	9	9	10.0%	18.2%	(B2.2.7)
Comm. on Defence Procurement	1	13	0	1	1	12	0.0%	7.7%	(B2.2.8)
1978 Parl. Comm. on Defence Policy	32	51	5	5	27	46	15.6%	9.8%	(B2.2.9)
Comm. on Certain Matters Pertaining to Military Intelligence	4	4	0	0	4	4	0.0%	0.0%	(B2.2.10)
Comm. for Coord. of New System of Ranks	10	10	0	1	10	9	0.0%	10.0%	(B2.2.11)
Comm. for a Cont. Review of Particip. of Women in Defence	8	14	2	5	6	9	25.0%	35.7%	(B2.2.12)
1979 Materiel Procurement Committee	3	26	0	2	3	24	0.0%	7.7%	(B2.2.13)
Comm. on Operat. Command of Def. Forces	11	19	0	1	11	18	0.0%	5.3%	(B2.2.14)
Comm. on Peacetime Org. of Def. Forces	14	19	0	1	14	18	0.0%	5.3%	(B2.2.15)
1974 Parl. Comm. on Defence Policy	24	22	1	1	23	21	4.2%	4.5%	(B2.2.16)
1973 Alternative Military Service Comm.	7	11	0	0	7	11	0.0%	0.0%	(B2.2.17)
1974 Comm. on Intelligence Questions	10	10	1	1	9	9	10.0%	10.0%	(B2.2.18)
Expert Studies Conc. Dev. after 1977 of Parts of Su.'s tot. Defence etc.	2	2	0	0	2	2	0.0%	0.0%	(B2.2.19)
Expert Study of Price Regulation	10	10	0	0	10	10	0.0%	0.0%	(B2.2.20)
1969 Comm. on Defence Research	16	17	0	1	16	16	0.0%	5.9%	(B2.2.21)
1970 Parl. Comm. on Defence Policy	19	21	0	0	19	21	0.0%	0.0%	(B2.2.22)
1965 Parl. Comm. on Defence Policy	26	28	1	0	25	28	3.8%	0.0%	(B2.2.23)
NUMBER OF COMM.MEMBERS/MIN. OF DEFENCE	**267**	**355**	**16**	**27**	**251**	**328**	**6.0%**	**7.6%**	

Table 3b: MINISTERIAL COMMITTEES SUBORDINATED TO MINISTRY FOR FOREIGN AFFAIRS:

NAME OF COMMITTEE	Start	End	Women Start	Women End	Men Start	Men End	%W Start	%W End	No of table
Delegation of Disarmament ***	24	31	4	6	20	25	16.7%	19.4%	(C3.1)
Su. Intern. Humanitarian Law. Del. ***	17	17	1	0	16	17	5.9%	0.0%	(C3.1)
Comm. on Sud. Act. abroad in Mil Equipm.	5	5	1	1	4	4	20.0%	20.0%	(D2.2.1)
Expert Study on Rel. Disarm. - Developm.	17	14	3	2	14	12	17.6%	14.3%	(D2.2.2)
South Africa Committee	12	17	2	2	10	15	16.7%	11.8%	(D2.2.3)
Comm. on the Future Act. of SIPRI	12	18	1	2	11	16	8.3%	11.1%	(D2.2.4)
Comm. on Concessionary Credits	5	8	0	0	5	8	0.0%	0.0%	(D2.2.5)
Su. Prep. Comm. for UN Conf. on Science and Technology for Development	22	23	3	3	19	20	13.6%	13.0%	(D2.2.6)
Comm. on Su.'s Intern. Dev. Cooperation	13	16	2	3	11	13	15.4%	18.8%	(D2.2.7)
Nat. Coord. Comm. for UN World Pop. Conf	15	24	3	4	12	20	20.0%	16.7%	(D2.2.8)
Comm. for Review of Su. Bilat. Measures for Promotion of Industr. of Dev. C.	5	8	0	0	5	8	0.0%	0.0%	(D2.2.9)
Comm. on Nordic Organizational Matters	3	3	0	0	3	3	0.0%	0.0%	(D2.2.10)
Exp. Study on Long-term Planf. Dev. Ass	1	1	0	0	1	1	0.0%	0.0%	(D2.2.11)
Working Group on International Develop- ment-Assistance Questions	25	23	4	3	21	20	16.0%	13.0%	(D2.2.12)
Comm. on the Position of Women	1	1	1	1	0	0	100.0%	100.0%	(D2.2.13)
Comm. on an International Peace and Conflict Research Inst. in Sweden	8	8	1	1	7	7	12.5%	12.5%	(D2.2.14)
NUMBER OF COMM.MEMB./MIN. F FOREIGN AFF.	**185**	**217**	**26**	**28**	**159**	**189**	**14.1%**	**12.9%**	
TOTAL NUMBER OF MEMBERS	**452**	**572**	**42**	**55**	**410**	**517**	**9.3%**	**9.6%**	

* Including permanent members, advisers, experts and secretariate. For details, see following tables.

** See explanation first in App. 2B. Notice that the Committees did not start and end at the same time. See each table.

*** These two Committees have become permanent authorities. For details, see App. 3A, page 4.

App. 28,
Page 4,
Summary.

TABLE 4: SUMMARY OF TOTAL NUMBER OF MEMBERS IN MINISTERIAL COMMITTEES, BY POSITION AND SEX.

Table 4a: Ministerial Committees subordinated to the Ministry of Defence.

	Permanent		Special Advisers		Experts		Secretariate		TOTAL	
	Start	End	Start	End	Start	End	Start	End	Start	End
WOMEN	7	14	3	3	4	7	2	3	16	27
MEN	74	96	44	28	95	153	38	51	251	328
TOTAL	81	110	47	31	99	160	40	54	267	355
% OF TOTAL										
WOMEN	8.6%	12.7%	6.4%	9.7%	4.0%	4.4%	5.0%	5.6%	6.0%	7.6%
MEN	91.4%	87.3%	93.6%	90.3%	96.0%	95.6%	95.0%	94.4%	94.0%	92.4%

Table 4b: Ministerial Committees subordinated to the Ministry for Foreign Affairs.*

	Permanent		Special Advisers		Experts		Secretariate		TOTAL	
	Start	End	Start	End	Start	End	Start	End	Start	End
WOMEN	17	18	4	2	4	7	1	1	26	28
MEN	73	89	41	32	19	47	26	21	159	189
TOTAL	90	107	45	34	23	54	27	22	185	217
% OF TOTAL										
WOMEN	18.9%	16.8%	8.9%	5.9%	17.4%	13.0%	3.7%	4.5%	14.1%	12.9%
MEN	81.1%	83.2%	91.1%	94.1%	82.6%	87.0%	96.3%	95.5%	85.9%	87.1%

* Notice that figures in table 4b include also the Delegation of Disarmament (see App. 3A, table C3.1) and Swedish International Humanitarian Law Delegation (see App. 3A, table D3.1).

MEMBERS OF THE MINISTERIAL COMMITTEES, BY POSITION AND SEX.

<B2.2> MINISTERIAL COMMITTEES SUBORDINATED TO THE MINISTRY OF DEFENCE.

<B2.2.1> 1984 PARLIAMENTARY COMMITTEE ON DEFENCE POLICY (1984 års försvarskommité)

The period during which the ministerial committee worked:
March 28, 1984 - December 1986.

The members of the committee by position and sex:

	Permanent		Special Advisers		Experts		Secretariate		TOTAL	
	Start	End	Start	End	Start	End	Start	End	Start	End
WOMEN	1	1	0	1	0	0	0	0	1	2
MEN	6	6	5	5	5	6	1	3	17	20
TOTAL	7	7	5	6	5	6	1	3	18	22
% OF TOTAL										
WOMEN	14.3%	14.3%	0.0%	16.7%	0.0%	0.0%	0.0%	0.0%	5.6%	9.1%
MEN	85.7%	85.7%	100.0%	83.3%	100.0%	100.0%	100.0%	100.0%	94.4%	90.9%

Source: Start: Kommittéberättelsen 1985, page 73.
End: Kommittéberättelsen 1987, page 52-53.

A Parliamentary appointed committee.
The woman was not the Chairperson.

<B2.2.2> COMMITTEE ON THE SUPREME OPERATIONAL COMMAND IN EMERGENCIES AND WAR (Ledningsverksamhetsutredningen)

The period during which the ministerial committee worked:
January 1, 1984 - December 1986.

The members of the committee by position and sex:

	Permanent		Special Advisers		Experts		Secretariate		TOTAL	
	Start	End	Start	End	Start	End	Start	End	Start	End
WOMEN	0	0	0	0	0	0	1	1	1	1
MEN	1	1	2	2	2	2	1	1	6	6
TOTAL	1	1	2	2	2	2	2	2	7	7
% OF TOTAL										
WOMEN	0.0%	0.0%	0.0%	0.0%	0.0%	0.0%	50.0%	50.0%	14.3%	14.3%
MEN	100.0%	100.0%	100.0%	100.0%	100.0%	100.0%	50.0%	50.0%	85.7%	85.7%

Source: Start: Kommittéberättelsen 1985, page 71-72.
End: Kommittéberättelsen 1987, page 50.

A One person committee.
The woman in the Secr. was
a Deputy secretary.

<B2.2.3> EXPERT STUDY ON RESISTANCE QUESTIONS (Motståndsutredningen)

The period during which the ministerial committee worked:
December 18, 1980 - June 14, 1984.

The members of the committee by position and sex:

	Permanent		Special Advisers		Experts		Secretariate		TOTAL	
	Start	End	Start	End	Start	End	Start	End	Start	End
WOMEN	0	0	0	0	1	1	1	1	2	2
MEN	1	1	0	0	4	4	1	1	6	6
TOTAL	1	1	0	0	5	5	2	2	8	8
% OF TOTAL										
WOMEN	0.0%	0.0%	-	-	20.0%	20.0%	50.0%	50.0%	25.0%	25.0%
MEN	100.0%	100.0%	-	-	80.0%	80.0%	50.0%	50.0%	75.0%	75.0%

Source: Start: Kommittéberättelsen 1982, page 72.
End: Kommittéberättelsen 1985, page 57-58.

A One person committee.
The woman in the Secr.
was a Deputy secretary.

(B2.2.4) SWEDISH INTERNATIONAL HUMANITARIAN LAW COMMITTEE (Folkrättskommittén)

The period during which the ministerial committee worked:
June 29, 1978 - August 31, 1984.

The members of the committee by position and sex:

	Permanent		Special Advisers		Experts		Secretariate		TOTAL	
	Start	End	Start	End	Start	End	Start	End	Start	End
WOMEN	0	0	0	0	0	1	0	0	0	1
MEN	6	6	9	8	3	3	2	2	17	19
TOTAL	6	6	9	8		4	2	2	17	20
% OF TOTAL										
WOMEN	0.0%	0.0%	0.0%	0.0%	-	25.0%	0.0%	0.0%	0.0%	5.0%
MEN	100.0%	100.0%	100.0%	100.0%	-	75.0%	100.0%	100.0%	100.0%	95.0%

Source: Start: Kommittéberättelsen 1979, page 79-80.
End: Kommittéberättelsen 1985, page 55-56.

A Civil servant committee

(B2.2.5) SUBMARINE DEFENCE COMMITTEE (Ubåtsskyddskommissionen)

The period during which the ministerial committee worked:
October 21, 1982 - December 1983.

The members of the committee by position and sex:

	Permanent		Special Advisers		Experts		Secretariate		TOTAL	
	Start	End	Start	End	Start	End	Start	End	Start	End
WOMEN	1	1	0	0	0	0	0	0	1	1
MEN	4	4	0	0	2	2	1	1	7	7
TOTAL	5	5	0	0	2	2	1	1	8	8
% OF TOTAL										
WOMEN	20.0%	20.0%	-	-	0.0%	0.0%	0.0%	0.0%	12.5%	12.5%
MEN	80.0%	80.0%	-	-	100.0%	100.0%	100.0%	100.0%	87.5%	87.5%

Source: Start: Kommittéberättelsen 1983, page 74.
End: Kommittéberättelsen 1984, page 83-84.

A parliamentary appointed committee
The woman was not the chairperson.

(B2.2.6) COMMITTEE ON THE OPERATIONAL COMMAND OF THE TOTAL DEFENCE ORGANIZATION IN THE CABINET OFFICE AND MINISTRIES (Utredningen om totalförsvarets ledning i regeringskansliet)

The period during which the ministerial committee worked:
September 16, 1982 - December 1983.

The members of the committee by position and sex:

	Permanent		Special Advisers		Experts		Secretariate		TOTAL	
	Start	End	Start	End	Start	End	Start	End	Start	End
WOMEN	0	0	0	0	0	0	0	0	0	0
MEN	1	1	0	0	0	0	1	1	2	2
TOTAL	1	1	0	0	0	0	1	1	2	2
% OF TOTAL										
WOMEN	0.0%	0.0%	-	-	-	-	0.0%	0.0%	0.0%	0.0%
MEN	100.0%	100.0%	-	-	-	-	100.0%	100.0%	100.0%	100.0%

Source: Start: Kommittéberättelsen 1983, page 73.
End: Kommittéberättelsen 1984, page 82.

A One person committee

<B2.2.7> COMMITTEE FOR PLANNING AND INFORMATION FOR PSYCHOLOGICAL DEFENCE
(Informationsberedskapsutredningen)

The period during which the ministerial committee worked:
March 12, 1981 - December 1983.

The members of the committee by position and sex:

	Permanent		Special Advisers		Experts		Secretariate		TOTAL	
	Start	End	Start	End	Start	End	Start	End	Start	End
WOMEN	0	1	0	0	1	1	0	0	1	2
MEN	1	3	0	0	7	5	1	1	9	9
TOTAL	1	4	0	0	8	6	1	1	10	11
% OF TOTAL										
WOMEN	0.0%	25.0%	--	--	12.5%	16.7%	0.0%	0.0%	10.0%	18.2%
MEN	100.0%	100.0%	--	--	87.5%	83.3%	100.0%	100.0%	90.0%	81.8%

A One person committee ("Start")
A Civil servant committee ("End")
The woman was not the chairperson.

Source: Start: Kommittéberättelsen 1982, page 72-.
End: Kommittéberättelsen 1984, page 68-69.

<B2.2.8> COMMITTEE ON DEFENCE PROCUREMENT (Utredningen om försvarsupphandling)

The period during which the ministerial committee worked:
October 30, 1980 - December 1983.

The members of the committee by position and sex:

	Permanent		Special Advisers		Experts		Secretariate		TOTAL	
	Start	End	Start	End	Start	End	Start	End	Start	End
WOMEN	0	0	0	0	0	1	0	0	0	1
MEN	1	1	0	0	10	10	0	1	11	12
TOTAL	1	1	0	0	10	11	0	1	11	13
% OF TOTAL										
WOMEN	0.0%	0.0%	--	--	--	9.1%	--	0.0%	0.0%	7.7%
MEN	100.0%	100.0%	--	--	--	90.9%	--	100.0%	100.0%	92.3%

A One person committee.

Source: Start: Kommittéberättelsen 1981, page 81.
End: Kommittéberättelsen 1984, page 67.

<B2.2.9> 1978 PARLIAMENTARY COMMITTEE ON DEFENCE POLICY (1978 års försvarskommitté)

The period during which the ministerial committee worked:
March 30, 1978 - December 1982.

The members of the committee by position and sex:

	Permanent		Special Advisers		Experts		Secretariate		TOTAL	
	Start	End	Start	End	Start	End	Start	End	Start	End
WOMEN	3	4	0	0	2	1	0	0	5	5
MEN	10	8	0	0	13	30	4	8	27	46
TOTAL	13	12	0	0	15	31	4	8	32	51
% OF TOTAL										
WOMEN	23.1%	33.3%	--	--	13.3%	3.2%	0.0%	0.0%	15.6%	9.8%
MEN	76.9%	66.7%	--	--	86.7%	96.8%	100.0%	100.0%	84.4%	90.2%

A parliamentary appointed committee.
None of the women was the chairperson.
The Experts "Start" were appointed
later than the Permanent members.
9 (incl. 1 woman) were appointed
in April 1978, 6 (incl. 1 woman)
were appointed in June 1978.

Source: Start: Kommittéberättelsen 1979, page 75-77.
End: Kommittéberättelsen 1983, page 55-57.

(B2.2.10) COMMITTEE ON CERTAIN MATTERS PERTAINING TO MILITARY INTELLIGENCE
(Kommittén om vissa frågor rörande den militära underrättelsetjänsten)

The period during which the ministerial committee worked:
June 21, 1979 - December 19, 1981.

The members of the committee by position and sex:

	Permanent		Special Advisers		Experts		Secretariate		TOTAL	
	Start	End	Start	End	Start	End	Start	End	Start	End
WOMEN	0	0	0	0	0	0	0	0	0	0
MEN	3	3	0	0	0	0	1	1	4	4
TOTAL	3	3	0	0	0	0	1	1	4	4
% OF TOTAL										
WOMEN	0.0%	0.0%	--	--	--	--			0.0%	0.0%
MEN	100.0%	100.0%							100.0%	100.0%

A Civil servant committee

Source: Start: Kommittéberättelsen 1980, page 36.
End: Kommittéberättelsen 1982, page 66.

(B2.2.11) COMMISSION FOR THE COORDINATION OF THE NEW SYSTEM OF RANKS IN THE DEFENCE FORCES (Delegationen för samordning av en ny befälsordning)

The period during which the ministerial committee worked:
June 1, 1978 - October 1981.

The members of the committee by position and sex:

	Permanent		Special Advisers		Experts		Secretariate		TOTAL	
	Start	End	Start	End	Start	End	Start	End	Start	End
WOMEN	0	1	0	0	0	0	0	0	0	1
MEN	9	8	0	0	0	0	1	1	10	9
TOTAL	9	9	0	0	0	0	1	1	10	10
% OF TOTAL										
WOMEN	0.0%	11.1%	--	--					0.0%	10.0%
MEN	100.0%	88.9%							100.0%	90.0%

A Civil servant committee.
The woman was not the Chairperson.

Source: Start: Kommittéberättelsen 1979, page 77.
End: Kommittéberättelsen 1982, page 63.

(B2.2.12) COMMITTEE FOR A CONTINUED REVIEW OF PARTICIPATION OF WOMEN IN THE DEFENCE FORCES (Beredningen för det fortsatta arbetet om kvinnan i försvaret)

The period during which the ministerial committee worked:
February 27, 1975 - December 17, 1980.

The members of the committee by position and sex:

	Permanent		Special Advisers		Experts		Secretariate		TOTAL	
	Start	End	Start	End	Start	End	Start	End	Start	End
WOMEN	1	4	1	1	0	1	0	0	2	5
MEN	0	2	1	1	5	6	0	1	6	9
TOTAL	1	6	2	2	5	7	0	1	8	14
% OF TOTAL										
WOMEN	100.0%	66.7%	50.0%	50.0%	0.0%	14.3%	--		25.0%	35.7%
MEN	0.0%	33.3%	50.0%	50.0%	100.0%	85.7%	--		75.0%	64.3%

A One person committee ("Start").
A Civil servant committee ("End").
A woman was the Special Investigator and the Chairperson at "Start" and "End", respectively.

Source: Start: Kommittéberättelsen 1976, page 132.
End: Kommittéberättelsen 1981, page 66-67.

(B2.2.13) 1979 MATERIEL PROCUREMENT COMMITTEE (1979 års materialanskaffningskommitté)

The period during which the ministerial committee worked:
September 13, 1979 - October 14, 1980.

The members of the committee by position and sex:

	Permanent Start	End	Special Advisers Start	End	Experts Start	End	Secretariate Start	End	TOTAL Start	End	
WOMEN	0	0	0	1	0	0	0	1	0	2	A One person committee.
MEN	1	1	6	7	0	14	2	2	9	24	The woman in the Secr. was a deputy secretary.
TOTAL	1	1	6	8	0	14	2	3	9	26	
% OF TOTAL											
WOMEN	0.0%	0.0%	0.0%	12.5%	-	0.0%	0.0%	33.3%	0.0%	7.7%	
MEN	100.0%	100.0%	100.0%	87.5%	-	100.0%	100.0%	66.7%	100.0%	92.3%	

Source: Start: Kommittéberättelsen 1980, page 87-88.
End: Kommittéberättelsen 1981, page 78-80.

(B2.2.14) COMMITTEE ON THE OPERATIONAL COMMAND OF THE DEFENCE FORCES (Försvarsmaktens ledningsutredning)

The period during which the ministerial committee worked:
September 20, 1974 - November 30, 1979.

The members of the committee by position and sex:

	Permanent Start	End	Special Advisers Start	End	Experts Start	End	Secretariate Start	End	TOTAL Start	End	
WOMEN	0	0	0	0	0	0	0	0	0	0	A One person committee ("Start").
MEN	1	7	5	0	4	10	1	2	11	19	A Parliamentary appointed committee ("End").
TOTAL	1	7	5	0	4	10	1	2	11	19	
% OF TOTAL											
WOMEN	0.0%	0.0%	0.0%	0.0%	0.0%	0.0%	0.0%	0.0%	0.0%	0.0%	
MEN	100.0%	100.0%	100.0%	100.0%	100.0%	100.0%	100.0%	100.0%	100.0%	100.0%	

Source: Start: Kommittéberättelsen 1975, page 177.
End: Kommittéberättelsen 1980, page 72-73.

(B2.2.15) COMMITTEE ON THE PEACETIME ORGANIZATION OF THE DEFENCE FORCES (Försvarets fredsorganisationsutredning)

The period during which the ministerial committee worked:
February 3, 1967 - June 5, 1978.

The members of the committee by position and sex:

	Permanent Start	End	Special Advisers Start	End	Experts Start	End	Secretariate Start	End	TOTAL Start	End	
WOMEN	0	1	0	0	0	0	0	0	0	1	A One person committee ("Start").
MEN	1	5	0	0	12	11	1	2	14	18	A Parliamentary appointed committee ("End").
TOTAL	1	6	0	0	12	11	1	2	14	19	The woman was not the chairperson.
% OF TOTAL											
WOMEN	0.0%	16.7%	-	-	0.0%	0.0%	0.0%	0.0%	0.0%	5.3%	
MEN	100.0%	83.3%	-	-	100.0%	100.0%	100.0%	100.0%	100.0%	94.7%	

Source: Start: Riksdagsberättelsen 1969, page 102.
End: Kommittéberättelsen 1979, page 65-66.

(B2.2.16) 1974 PARLIAMENTARY COMMITTEE ON DEFENCE POLICY (1974 års försvarsutredning).

The period during which the ministerial committee worked:
October 25, 1974 - January 25, 1977.

The members of the committee by position and sex:

	Permanent		Special Advisers		Experts		Secretariate		TOTAL	
	Start	End	Start	End	Start	End	Start	End	Start	End
WOMEN	0	1	1	1	0	0	0	0	1	1
MEN	1	6	5	0	12	11	5	4	23	21
TOTAL	1	7	6	0	12	11	5	4	24	22
% OF TOTAL										
WOMEN	0.0%	14.3%	16.7%	-	0.0%	0.0%	0.0%	0.0%	4.2%	4.5%
MEN	100.0%	85.7%	83.3%	-	100.0%	100.0%	100.0%	100.0%	95.8%	95.5%

Source: Start: Kommittéberättelsen 1975, page 181-182.
End: Kommittéberättelsen 1978, page 68-69.

A One person committee ("Start", all Spec. Adv. were Members of Parliament).
A Parliamentary appointed committee ("End").
Four of the secretaries at "Start" were appointed in November 1974, all of them were deputy secretaries.
The female permanent member was not the chairperson.

(B2.2.17) 1973 ALTERNATIVE MILITARY SERVICE COMMITTEE (1973 års utredning för översyn av lagen om vapenfri tjänst, vapenfriutredningen)

The period during which the ministerial committee worked:
September 13, 1973 - March 1977.

The members of the committee by position and sex:

	Permanent		Special Advisers		Experts		Secretariate		TOTAL	
	Start	End	Start	End	Start	End	Start	End	Start	End
WOMEN	0	0	0	0	0	0	0	0	0	0
MEN	1	6	5	0	0	2	1	3	7	11
TOTAL	1	6	5	0	0	2	1	3	7	11
% OF TOTAL										
WOMEN	0.0%	0.0%	0.0%	-	-	0.0%	0.0%	0.0%	0.0%	0.0%
MEN	100.0%	100.0%	100.0%	-	-	100.0%	100.0%	100.0%	100.0%	100.0%

Source: Start: Riksdagsberättelsen 1974, page 152.
End: Kommittéberättelsen 1978, page 66-67.

A One person committee ("Start").
A Civil servant committee ("End").

(B2.2.18) 1974 COMMITTEE ON INTELLIGENCE QUESTIONS (1974 års underrättelseutredning)

The period during which the ministerial committee worked:
January 4, 1974 - January 15, 1976.

The members of the committee by position and sex:

	Permanent		Special Advisers		Experts		Secretariate		TOTAL	
	Start	End	Start	End	Start	End	Start	End	Start	End
WOMEN	0	0	1	1	0	0	0	0	1	1
MEN	1	1	4	4	2	2	2	2	9	9
TOTAL	1	1	5	5	2	2	2	2	10	10
% OF TOTAL										
WOMEN	0.0%	0.0%	20.0%	20.0%	0.0%	0.0%	0.0%	0.0%	10.0%	10.0%
MEN	100.0%	100.0%	80.0%	80.0%	100.0%	100.0%	100.0%	100.0%	90.0%	90.0%

Source: Start: Kommittéberättelsen 1975, page 170-171.
End: Kommittéberättelsen 1977, page 65.

A One man committee.

App. B8.
Page 11.

(B2.2.19) EXPERT STUDIES CONCERNING THE DEVELOPMENT AFTER 1977 OF THE PARTS OF SWEDEN'S TOTAL
DEFENCE THAT ARE NOT INCL. IN MILITARY DEFENCE, CIVIL DEFENCE AND ECONOMIC DEFENCE
(Sakkunnig för studier avsende utv. efter 1977 av de delar av tot.försv. som inte
omfattas av mil. försvar, civilförsvar och ek. försvar)

The period during which the ministerial committee worked:
December 20, 1973 - December 1975.

The members of the committee by position and sex:

| | Permanent | | Special Advisers | | Experts | | Secretariate | | TOTAL | |
	Start	End	Start	End	Start	End	Start	End	Start	End
WOMEN	0	0	0	0	0	0	0	0	0	0
MEN	1	1	0	0	0	0	0	1	2	2
TOTAL	1	1	0	0	0	0	0	1	2	2
% OF TOTAL										
WOMEN	0.0%	0.0%	-	-	-	-	0.0%	0.0%	0.0%	0.0%
MEN	100.0%	100.0%	-	-	-	-	100.0%	100.0%	100.0%	100.0%

A One man committee.

Source: Start: Kommittéberättelsen 1975, page 168.
End: Kommittéberättelsen 1976, page 124.

(B2.2.20) EXPERT STUDY OF THE PRICE REGULATION OF DEFENCE EXPENDITURE
(Expertutredningen ang. prisregleringen av försvarsutgifterna)

The period during which the ministerial committee worked:
May 17, 1974 - April 7, 1975.

The members of the committee by position and sex:

| | Permanent | | Special Advisers | | Experts | | Secretariate | | TOTAL | |
	Start	End	Start	End	Start	End	Start	End	Start	End
WOMEN	0	0	0	0	0	0	0	0	0	0
MEN	1	1	2	2	6	6	1	1	10	10
TOTAL	1	1	2	2	6	6	1	1	10	10
% OF TOTAL										
WOMEN	0.0%	0.0%	0.0%	0.0%	0.0%	0.0%	0.0%	0.0%	0.0%	0.0%
MEN	100.0%	100.0%	100.0%	100.0%	100.0%	100.0%	100.0%	100.0%	100.0%	100.0%

A One man committee.

Source: Start: Kommittéberättelsen 1975, page 174-175.
End: Kommittéberättelsen 1976, page 125-126.

(B2.2.21) 1969 COMMITTEE ON DEFENCE RESEARCH (1969 års försvarsforskningsutr.)

The period during which the ministerial committee worked:
February 14, 1969 - October 1972.

The members of the committee by position and sex:

| | Permanent | | Special Advisers | | Experts | | Secretariate | | TOTAL | |
	Start	End	Start	End	Start	End	Start	End	Start	End
WOMEN	0	0	0	0	0	1	0	0	0	1
MEN	5	5	0	0	3	8	2	3	10	16
TOTAL	5	5	0	0	3	9	2	3	10	17
% OF TOTAL										
WOMEN	0.0%	0.0%	-	-	0.0%	11.1%	0.0%	0.0%	0.0%	5.9%
MEN	100.0%	100.0%	-	-	100.0%	88.9%	100.0%	100.0%	100.0%	94.1%

A Civil servant committee.

Source: Start: Riksdagsberättelsen 1970, page 111.
End: Riksdagsberättelsen 1973, page 116.

(B2.2.22) 1970 PARLIAMENTARY COMMITTEE ON DEFENCE POLICY (1970 års försvarsutredning)
==
The period during which the ministerial committee worked:
October 16, 1970 - May 1972.

The members of the committee by position and sex:

	Permanent		Special Advisers		Experts		Secretariate		TOTAL	
	Start	End	Start	End	Start	End	Start	End	Start	End
WOMEN	0	0	0	0	0	0	0	0	0	0
MEN	6	6	0	0	9	10	4	5	19	21
TOTAL	6	6	0	0	9	10	4	5	19	21
% OF TOTAL										
WOMEN	0.0%	0.0%	--	--	0.0%	0.0%	0.0%	0.0%	0.0%	0.0%
MEN	100.0%	100.0%	--	--	100.0%	100.0%	100.0%	100.0%	100.0%	100.0%

Source: Start: Riksdagsberättelsen 1971, page 109.
End: Riksdagsberättelsen 1973, page 119-120.

A parliamentary appointed committee.

(B2.2.23) 1965 PARLIAMENTARY COMMITTEE ON DEFENCE POLICY (1965 års försvarsutredning)
==
The period during which the ministerial committee worked:
January 29, 1965 - February 21, 1968.

The members of the committee by position and sex:

	Permanent		Special Advisers		Experts		Secretariate		TOTAL	
	Start	End	Start	End	Start	End	Start	End	Start	End
WOMEN	1	0	0	0	0	0	0	0	1	0
MEN	12	13	0	0	9	11	4	4	25	28
TOTAL	13	13	0	0	9	11	4	4	26	28
% OF TOTAL										
WOMEN	7.7%	0.0%	--	--	0.0%	0.0%	0.0%	0.0%	3.8%	0.0%
MEN	92.3%	100.0%	--	--	100.0%	100.0%	100.0%	100.0%	96.2%	100.0%

Source: Start: Riksdagsberättelsen 1966, page 114.
End: Riksdagsberättelsen 1969, page 90-91.

A parliamentary appointed committee.
The Experts "Start" were appointed in
April 1965 (6 persons) and November
1965 (3 persons). The Secretaries
"Start" were appointed in February
(1 person) and September 1965 (2 persons).
The woman was not the chairman.

(D2.2) MINISTERIAL COMMITTEES SUBORDINATED TO THE MINISTRY FOR FOREIGN AFFAIRS.
===

See tables C3.1 and D3.1 in Appendix 3A for information about two
committees which have become permanent authorities.

(D2.2.1) COMMITTEE ON SWEDISH ACTIVITIES ABROAD IN THE MILITARY EQUIPMENT SECTOR
(Utredningen om svensk utlandsverksamhet på krigsmaterielområdet)
===

The period during which the ministerial committee worked:
June 19, 1985 - Figures shows December 1986. (The investigation continued its work during 1987.)

The members of the committee by position and sex:

	Permanent Start	End	Special Advisers Start	End	Experts Start	End	Secretariate Start	End	TOTAL Start	End	
WOMEN	0	0	0	0	1	1	0	0	1	1	A
MEN	1	1	0	0	2	2	1	1	4	4	
TOTAL	1	1	0	0	3	3	1	1	5	5	
% OF TOTAL											
WOMEN	0.0%	0.0%	-	-	33.3%	33.3%	0.0%	0.0%	20.0%	20.0%	
MEN	100.0%	100.0%	-	-	66.7%	66.7%	100.0%	100.0%	80.0%	80.0%	

A One person committee.

Source: Start: Kommittéberättelsen 1986, page 46.
End: Kommittéberättelsen 1987, page 43.

(D2.2.2) EXPERT STUDY ON THE RELATIONSHIP BETWEEN DISARMAMENT AND DEVELOPMENT
(Utredningen om samband mellan nedrustning och utveckling)
===

The period during which the ministerial committee worked:
July 14, 1983 - December 1985.

The members of the committee by position and sex:

	Permanent Start	End	Special Advisers Start	End	Experts Start	End	Secretariate Start	End	TOTAL Start	End	
WOMEN	1	1	1	1	1	0	0	0	3	2	A
MEN	0	0	11	11	0	0	3	1	14	12	B
TOTAL	1	1	12	12	1	0	3	1	17	14	C
% OF TOTAL											
WOMEN	100.0%	100.0%	8.3%	8.3%	100.0%	-	0.0%	0.0%	17.6%	14.3%	
MEN	0.0%	0.0%	91.7%	91.7%	0.0%	-	100.0%	100.0%	82.4%	85.7%	

A One person committee.
B The Expert at "Start" was
appointed October 1, 1983.
C One person in the Secretariate at "Start" was
appointed October 1, 1983.

Source: Start: Kommittéberättelsen 1984, page 62.
End: Kommittéberättelsen 1986, page 44.

(C2.2.3) SOUTH AFRICA COMMITTEE (Sydafrikakommittén)

The period during which the ministerial committee worked:
October 30, 1980 - December 1984.

The members of the committee by position and sex:

	Permanent Start	End	Special Advisers Start	End	Experts Start	End	Secretariate Start	End	TOTAL Start	End
WOMEN	1	1	0	0	0	0	1	1	2	2
MEN	4	6	2	2	2	5	2	2	10	15
TOTAL	5	7	2	2	2	5	3	3	12	17
% OF TOTAL										
WOMEN	20.0%	14.3%	0.0%	0.0%	0.0%	0.0%	33.3%	33.3%	16.7%	11.8%
MEN	80.0%	85.7%	100.0%	100.0%	100.0%	100.0%	66.7%	66.7%	83.3%	88.2%

Source: Start: Kommittéberättelsen 1984, page 57-58.
End: Kommittéberättelsen 1985, page 50-51.

A Parliamentary appointed committee.
The woman who was a permanent member was not the Chairperson.
The woman in the Secr. was a Deputy secretary.

(C2.2.4) COMMITTEE ON CONCESSIONARY CREDITS FOR DEVELOPMENT COUNTRIES (Utr. för utvärdering av system för förmånliga kreditgivning til U-länder)

The period during which the ministerial committee worked:
June 16, 1982 - December 1983.

The members of the committee by position and sex:

	Permanent Start	End	Special Advisers Start	End	Experts Start	End	Secretariate Start	End	TOTAL Start	End
WOMEN	0	0	1	1	0	1	0	0	1	2
MEN	1	1	8	11	1	2	1	2	11	16
TOTAL	1	1	9	12	1	3	1	2	12	18
% OF TOTAL										
WOMEN	0.0%	0.0%	11.1%	8.3%	0.0%	33.3%	0.0%	0.0%	8.3%	11.1%
MEN	100.0%	100.0%	88.9%	91.7%	100.0%	66.7%	100.0%	100.0%	91.7%	88.9%

Source: Start: Kommittéberättelsen 1983, page 53.
End: Kommittéberättelsen 1984, page 58-59.

A One person committee.

(C2.2.5) COMMISSION ON THE FUTURE ACTIVITIES OF THE STOCKHOLM INTERNATIONAL PEACE RESEARCH INSTITUE (Utr. om formerna för stiftelsen SIPRIs framtida verksamhet)

The period during which the ministerial committee worked:
May 11, 1978 - December 1979.

The members of the committee by position and sex:

	Permanent Start	End	Special Advisers Start	End	Experts Start	End	Secretariate Start	End	TOTAL Start	End
WOMEN	0	0	0	0	0	0	0	0	0	0
MEN	1	1	2	2	1	4	1	1	5	8
TOTAL	1	1	2	2	1	4	1	1	5	8
% OF TOTAL										
WOMEN	0.0%	0.0%	0.0%	0.0%	0.0%	0.0%	0.0%	0.0%	0.0%	0.0%
MEN	100.0%	100.0%	100.0%	100.0%	100.0%	100.0%	100.0%	100.0%	100.0%	100.0%

Source: Start: Kommittéberättelsen 1979, page 63.
End: Kommittéberättelsen 1980, page 66-67.

A One person committee.
All members at "Start" appointed in September 1978.

App. 18,
Page 15.

(D2.2.6) SWEDISH PREPARATORY COMMITTEE FOR THE UN CONFERENCE ON SCIENCE AND TECH-NOLOGY FOR DEVELOPMENT (Kommittén för de svenska förberedelserna inför FN:s konferens om vetenskap och teknologi för utveckling)

The period during which the ministerial committee worked:
May 26, 1977 - December 1979

The members of the committee by position and sex:

	Permanent Start	End	Special Advisers Start	End	Experts Start	End	Secretariate Start	End	TOTAL Start	End
WOMEN	3	3	0	0	0	0	0	0	3	3
MEN	17	18	2	0	0	0	2	2	19	20
TOTAL	20	21	0	0	0	0	2	2	22	23
% OF TOTAL										
WOMEN	15.0%	14.3%	-	-	-	-	0.0%	0.0%	13.6%	13.0%
MEN	85.0%	85.7%	-	-	-	-	100.0%	100.0%	86.4%	87.0%

Source: Start: Kommittéberättelsen 1978, page 61-62.
End: Kommittéberättelsen 1980, page 65-66.

A civil servant committee.
None of the women has the chairperson.
One person in the Secretariate at "Start" was also a Permanent member at "Start".

(D2.2.7) COMMISSION ON SWEDEN'S INTERNATIONAL DEVELOPMENT COOPERATION (Sakkunniga med uppdrag att företa en utredning ang. Sveriges utv.samarb. med U-länderna)

The period during which the ministerial committee worked:
December 8, 1972 - December 1978.

The members of the committee by position and sex:

	Permanent Start	End	Special Advisers Start	End	Experts Start	End	Secretariate Start	End	TOTAL Start	End
WOMEN	0	0	2	2	0	1	0	0	2	3
MEN	1	1	7	9	0	2	3	2	11	13
TOTAL	1	1	9	11	0	3	3	2	13	16
% OF TOTAL										
WOMEN	0.0%	0.0%	22.2%	18.2%	-	33.3%	0.0%	0.0%	15.4%	18.8%
MEN	100.0%	100.0%	77.8%	81.8%	-	66.7%	100.0%	100.0%	84.6%	81.3%

Source: Start: Riksdagsberättelsen 1974, page 131-132.
End: Kommittéberättelsen 1979, page 59.

A one person committee ("Start").
A Parliamentary appointed committee ("End").
None of the women has the chairperson.

(D2.2.8) NATIONAL COORDINATING COMMITTEE FOR THE UN WORLD POPULATION CONFERENCE (Nationalkommittén för FN:s befolkningskonferens)

The period during which the ministerial committee worked:
March 17, 1972 - December 1974.

The members of the committee by position and sex:

	Permanent Start	End	Special Advisers Start	End	Experts Start	End	Secretariate Start	End	TOTAL Start	End
WOMEN	3	3	0	0	0	1	0	0	3	4
MEN	10	10	0	0	0	8	2	2	12	20
TOTAL	13	13	0	0	0	9	2	2	15	24
% OF TOTAL										
WOMEN	23.1%	23.1%	-	-	-	11.1%	0.0%	0.0%	20.0%	16.7%
MEN	76.9%	76.9%	-	-	-	88.9%	100.0%	100.0%	80.0%	83.3%

Source: Start: Riksdagsberättelsen 1973, page 102-103.
End: Kommittéberättelsen 1975, page 147-148.

A civil servant committee.
One of the women has the chairperson.

**(D2.2.9) COMMITTEE FOR A REVIEW OF SWEDISH BILATERAL MAESURES FOR THE PROMOTION OF THE
INDUSTRIALIZATION OF THE DEVELOPING COUNTRIES <Sakkunniga för översyn av
svenska bilaterala åtgärder ägnade att främja U-ländernas industrialisering>**

The period during which the ministerial committee worked:
July 23, 1971 - December 1972.

The members of the committee by position and sex:

| | Permanent | | Special Advisers | | Experts | | Secretariate | | TOTAL | |
	Start	End	Start	End	Start	End	Start	End	Start	End
WOMEN	0	0	0	0	0	0.	0	0	0	0
MEN	1	1	3	5	0	0	1	2	5	8
TOTAL	1	1	3	5	0	0	1	2	5	8
% OF TOTAL										
WOMEN	0.0%	0.0%	0.0%	0.0%	-	-	0.0%	0.0%	0.0%	0.0%
MEN	100.0%	100.0%	100.0%	100.0%	-	-	100.0%	100.0%	100.0%	100.0%

A One person committee.

Source: Start: Riksdagsberättelsen 1972, page 92.
        End: Riksdagsberättelsen 1973, page 101.

(D2.2.10) COMMITTEE ON NORDIC ORGANIZATIONAL MATTERS <Nordiska organisationskommittén>

The period during which the ministerial committee worked:
November 24, 1967 - September 1970.

The members of the committee by position and sex:

| | Permanent | | Special Advisers | | Experts | | Secretariate | | TOTAL | |
	Start	End	Start	End	Start	End	Start	End	Start	End
WOMEN	0	0	0	0	0	0	0	0	0	0
MEN	1	1	1	1	0	0	1	1	3	3
TOTAL	1	1	1	1	0	0	1	1	3	3
% OF TOTAL										
WOMEN	0.0%	0.0%	-	-	-	-	0.0%	0.0%	0.0%	0.0%
MEN	100.0%	100.0%	-	-	-	-	100.0%	100.0%	100.0%	100.0%

A One person committee.

Source: Start: Riksdagsberättelsen 1963, page 87-88.
        End: Riksdagsberättelsen 1971, page 91.

**(D2.2.11) EXPERT STUDY ON A LONG-TERM PLAN FOR DEVELOPMENT ASSISTANCE
<Sakkunnig rörande långtidsplan för utvecklingsbiståndet>**

The period during which the ministerial committee worked:
November 24, 1967 - January 1969.

The members of the committee by position and sex:

| | Permanent | | Special Advisers | | Experts | | Secretariate | | TOTAL | |
	Start	End	Start	End	Start	End	Start	End	Start	End
WOMEN	0	0	0	0	0	0	0	0	0	0
MEN	1	1	0	0	0	0	0	0	1	1
TOTAL	1	1	0	0	0	0	0	0	1	1
% OF TOTAL										
WOMEN	0.0%	0.0%	-	-	-	-	-	-	0.0%	0.0%
MEN	100.0%	100.0%	-	-	-	-	-	-	100.0%	100.0%

A One person committee.

Source: Start: Riksdagsberättelsen 1968, page 85.
        End: Riksdagsberättelsen 1969, page 85.

<D2.2.12> WORKING-GROUP ON INTERNATIONAL DEVELOPMENT-ASSISTANCE QUESTIONS (Beredningen för internationella biståndsfrågor)

The period during which the ministerial committee worked:
February 10, 1961 - November 8, 1968.

The members of the committee by position and sex:

	Permanent		Special Advisers		Experts		Secretariate		TOTAL	
	Start	End	Start	End	Start	End	Start	End	Start	End
WOMEN	4	3	0	0	0	0	0	0	4	3
MEN	20	19	0	0	0	0	1	1	21	20
TOTAL	24	22	0	0	0	0	1	1	25	23
% OF TOTAL										
WOMEN	16.7%	13.6%	--	--	--	--	0.0%	0.0%	16.0%	13.0%
MEN	83.3%	86.4%	--	--	--	--	100.0%	100.0%	84.0%	87.0%

Source: Start: Riksdagsberättelsen 1962, page 66.
End: Riksdagsberättelsen 1969, page 85.

A Civil servant committee.
None of the women was the Chairperson.

<D2.2.13> COMMITTEE ON THE POSITION OF WOMEN (Utredning rörande kvinnans ställning)

The period during which the ministerial committee worked:
August 25, 1967 - July 1, 1968.

The members of the committee by position and sex:

	Permanent		Special Advisers		Experts		Secretariate		TOTAL	
	Start	End	Start	End	Start	End	Start	End	Start	End
WOMEN	1	1	0	0	0	0	0	0	1	1
MEN	0	0	0	0	0	0	0	0	0	0
TOTAL	1	1	0	0	0	0	0	0	1	1
% OF TOTAL										
WOMEN	100.0%	100.0%	--	--	--	--	--	--	100.0%	100.0%
MEN	0.0%	0.0%	--	--	--	--	--	--	0.0%	0.0%

Source: Start: Riksdagsberättelsen 1968, page 84.
End: Riksdagsberättelsen 1969, page 86.

A One person committee.

<D2.2.14> COMMITTEE ON AN INTERNATIONAL PEACE AND CONFLICT RESEARCH INSTITUTE IN SWEDEN (Fredsforskningsutredningen)

The period during which the ministerial committee worked:
December 11, 1964 - January 21, 1966.

The members of the committee by position and sex:

	Permanent		Special Advisers		Experts		Secretariate		TOTAL	
	Start	End	Start	End	Start	End	Start	End	Start	End
WOMEN	1	1	0	0	0	0	0	0	1	1
MEN	5	5	0	0	0	0	2	2	7	7
TOTAL	6	6	0	0	0	0	2	2	8	8
% OF TOTAL										
WOMEN	16.7%	16.7%	--	--	--	--	0.0%	0.0%	12.5%	12.5%
MEN	83.3%	83.3%	--	--	--	--	100.0%	100.0%	87.5%	87.5%

Source: Start: Riksdagsberättelsen 1966, page 93.
End: Riksdagsberättelsen 1967, page 107-108.

A Civil servant committee.
The woman was the Chairperson.

Appendix 3.

Statistical Data of the Representation of Women in Decision-Making Bodies within the Swedish Government Authorities.

Appendix 3A:
The Central Government Authorities.

Appendix 3B:
The Diplomatic Service and Swedish Delegations Abroad.

Information - Tables in Appendix 3A:

In some of the tables in Appendix 3A included persons are categorized, after their titles, into three categories:
Board
Advisers and
Officials responsible for processing issues ("Proc").

The titles changes, however, over time and it has in some cases been difficult to categorize the person after his/her title. I have therefore chosen to list, below each table, the titles (persons) included in each category.

SUMMARY OF DECISION-MAKING BODIES - THE CENTRAL GOVERNMENT AUTHORITIES.

TABLE 1: Defence Issues. Number of and Per Cent Women, by Year. All Included Officials*.

NAME OF DECISION-MAKING BODY	NUMBER OF WOMEN			PER CENT WOMEN			TOTAL NUMBER OF MEMBERS*			No of table
	1966/67	1976/77	1986/87	1966/67	1976/77	1986/87	1966/67	1976/77	1986/87	
Supreme Comm. / Defence Staff	0	0	1	0.0%	0.0%	1.9%	35	34	52	(B3.1)
Head of Army / Army Staff	0	0	1	0.0%	0.0%	2.8%	24	35	36	(B3.2)
Head of Nat. Home Guard/ NHG Staff	0	0	0	0.0%	0.0%	0.0%	6	6	6	(B3.3)
Head of Navy / Naval Staff	0	0	0	0.0%	0.0%	0.0%	23	26	27	(B3.4)
Head of Air Forces / Air Staff	0	0	0	0.0%	0.0%	0.0%	15	17	27	(B3.5)
Defence Materiel Adm. (FMV)	0	1	9	-	0.0%	5.0%		136	180	(B3.6)
National Board of Civil Def.	1	1	2	5.3%	5.9%	5.0%	19	34	40	(B3.7)
Nat. Board of Psychol. Def.	1	2	0	6.7%	11.8%	0.0%	15	17	9	(B3.8)
Nat. Board of Econ. Def.	0	0	5	0.0%	0.0%	10.9%	14	42	46	(B3.9)
Office of the Director, Regional Civilian Defence Area	0	0	0	0.0%		0.0%	12	12	17	(B3.10)
ALL DECISION-MAKING BODIES	2	4	18	1.2%	1.1%	4.1%	163	359	440	
ONLY THE ARMED FORCES	0	0	2		1.4%	4.2%	105	118	148	
ONLY BOARDS (not incl. FMV)	2	4	7	4.2%	4.3%	7.4%	48	93	95	

* Both men and women.

TABLE 2: Disarmament Issues. Number of and Per Cent Women, by Year. All Included Members*.

NAME OF DECISION-MAKING BODY	NUMBER OF WOMEN			PER CENT WOMEN			TOTAL NUMBER OF MEMBERS*			No of table
	1966/67	1976/77	1986/87	1966/67	1976/77	1986/87	1966/67	1976/77	1986/87	
The Delegation of Disarmament**	-	4	6	-	16.7%	19.4%	-	24	31	(C3.1)
ALL DECISION-MAKING BODIES	-	4	6	-	16.7%	19.4%	-	24	31	

* Both men and women.
** Figures show "Start" and "End". See explanation page 1, Appendix 2B and table C3.1.

TABLE 3: Issues concerning Foreign Affairs and Foreign Aid. Number of and Percent Women, by Year. All Included Officials*.

NAME OF DECISION-MAKING BODY	NUMBER OF WOMEN			PER CENT WOMEN			TOTAL NUMBER OF MEMBERS*			No of table
	1966/67	1976/77	1986/87	1966/67	1976/77	1986/87	1966/67	1976/77	1986/87	
Swedish International Humanitarian Law Delegation*		1	0		5.9%	0.0%		17	17	(D3.1)
Swedish International Dev. Author.	2	8	17	7.1%	16.3%	27.0%	28	49	63	(D3.2)
Swedish Board for Education in International Development		0	4		0.0%	40.0%		7	10	(D3.3)
Consultative Committee on Humanitarian Assistance	1	1	2	14.3%	10.0%	9.5%	7	10	21	(D3.4)
Advisory Council on Development Cooperation Issues		0	4		0.0%	30.8%		10	13	(D3.5)
ALL DECISION-MAKING BODIES	3	10	27	8.6%	10.8%	21.6%	35	93	124	

* Both men and women.
** Figures show "Start" and "End". See explanation page 1, Appendix 2B and table C3.1.

(B) DECISION-MAKING BODIES DEALING WITH DEFENCE ISSUES. (B3) CENTRAL GOVERNMENT AUTHORITIES (Authorities subordinated to the Ministry of Defence.)

(B3.1) THE SUPREME COMMANDER OF THE ARMED FORCES (incl. staff) AND DEFENCE STAFF. (överbefälhavaren och försvarsstab)

Total by year and sex.

	1966/67	1976/77	1986/87
WOMEN	0	0	1
MEN	35	34	51
TOTAL	35	34	52
% OF TOTAL			
WOMEN	0.0%	0.0%	1.9%
MEN	100.0%	100.0%	98.1%

Source: Sveriges Statskalender 1967, page 93-95.
Sveriges Statskalender 1977, page 91-92.
Sveriges Statskalender 1986, page 107-109.

The Supreme Commander of the Armed Forces (incl. staff) includes all three years 3 persons: the Supreme Commander and two assistants (adjutant och juridiskt biträde).

The Defence Staff includes the Head of the Defence Staff (försv.stabschef), the Deputy Head of the Defence Staff, Heads of Operations Directorate (operations-ledning), Planning Directorate (planeringsledning) and ADP Department (ADB-avdeln.), Senior Officers, Heads of Sections (sektionschefer) and Heads of Departments (avdelningschefer) (incl. the expert in disarmament issues).

The woman 1986/87 is Head of Library. (Head of Department)

(B3.2) THE HEAD OF THE ARMY (incl. staff) AND ARMY STAFF (Chefen för Armén och arméstab).

Total by year and sex.

	1966/67	1976/77	1986/87
WOMEN	0	0	1
MEN	24	35	35
TOTAL	24	35	36
% OF TOTAL			
WOMEN	0.0%	0.0%	2.8%
MEN	100.0%	100.0%	97.2%

Source: Sveriges Statskalender 1967, page 95-96.
Sveriges Statskalender 1977, page 93-94.
Sveriges Statskalender 1986, page 109-110.

The Head of the Army (incl. staff) includes: 1966/67 - only the Head of the Army; 1976/77 and 1986/87 - the Head of the Army and his assistant (adjutant).

The Army Staff includes the Head of the Army Staff (arméstabschef), Heads of Sections (sektionschefer), Service Branch Directors (truppslagsinspektörer) and Heads of Departments (avdelningschefer).

The woman 1986/87 is Head of the Central Office at the Administrative Department (centralexpedition på Adm. avd.).

(B3.3) THE HEAD OF THE NATIONAL HOME GUARD AND THE NATIONAL HOME GUARD STAFF (Hemvärnet).

Total by year and sex.

	1966/67	1976/77	1986/87
WOMEN	0	0	0
MEN	6	6	6
TOTAL	6	6	6
% OF TOTAL			
WOMEN	0.0%	0.0%	0.0%
MEN	100.0%	100.0%	100.0%

Source: Sveriges Statskalender 1967, page 96.
Sveriges Statskalender 1977, page 94-95.
Sveriges Statskalender 1986, page 110.

The Head of the National Home Guard: no staff included. The National Home Guard Staff includes the Head of the National Home Guard Staff (Rikshemv.chefen) and Heads of Departments (incl. Chief Inf. and Security Off.) (aud.chefer, inkl. Inf.& Säker-hetschef).

(B3.4) THE HEAD OF THE NAVY (incl. staff) AND THE NAVAL STAFF (Chefen för Marinen och Marinstab).

Total by year and sex.

	1966/67	1976/77	1986/87
WOMEN	0	0	0
MEN	23	26	27
TOTAL	23	26	27
% OF TOTAL			
WOMEN	0.0%	0.0%	0.0%
MEN	100.0%	100.0%	100.0%

Source: Sveriges Statskalender 1967, page 96-97.
Sveriges Statskalender 1977, page 95-96.
Sveriges Statskalender 1986, page 110-111.

The Head of the Navy (incl. staff) includes 2 persons: The Head of the Navy and his assistant (adjutant). The Naval Staff includes the Head of the Naval Staff (marinstabschef), Heads of Sections (sektionschefer) and Heads of Departments (aud.chefer).

(B3.5) THE HEAD OF THE AIR FORCES AND THE AIR STAFF (Chefen för flygvapnet och flygstab).

Total by year and sex.

	1966/67	1976/77	1986/87
WOMEN	0	0	0
MEN	15	17	27
TOTAL	15	17	27
% OF TOTAL			
WOMEN	0.0%	0.0%	0.0%
MEN	100.0%	100.0%	100.0%

Source: Sveriges Statskalender 1967, page 97.
Sveriges Statskalender 1977, page 96.
Sveriges Statskalender 1986, page 111-112.

The Head of the Air Forces: no staff included. The Air Staff includes the Head of the Air Staff, Heads of Sections and Heads of Departments (sektions- och aud.chefer, inkl. flygsäkerhetsavd.).

(B) DECISION-MAKING BODIES DEALING WITH DEFENCE ISSUES. (B3) CENTRAL GOVERNMENT AUTHORITIES (Authorities
subordinated to the Ministry of Defence.)

(B3.6) DEFENCE MATERIEL ADMINISTRATION.
(Försvarets materielverk. FMV)

Total by year and sex.

	1966/67	1976/77	1986/87
WOMEN	-	0	9
MEN	-	136	171
TOTAL	-	136	180
% OF TOTAL			
WOMEN	-	0.0%	5.0%
MEN	-	100.0%	95.0%

Source: Sveriges Statskalender 1977, page 102-113.
Sveriges Statskalender 1986, page 116-123.

This authority was established in 1968.
In table B3.6 the following are included:
The Board (incl. the Director-General (=the Chairperson),
3 repr. of the staff (personalföretr.)>, Heads of Divisions
(byråchefer samt chefer för huvudaud.)>, Heads of Departments
(aud.chefer samt chefer för underaud.) and Principal Adm.
Officers (Aud.dir samt chefer för enheter).

THE FOLLOWING AUTHORITIES ARE NOT INCLUDED IN THE ARMED FORCES.

(B3.7) NATIONAL BOARD OF CIVIL DEFENCE, RESCUE AND FIRE SERVICES (Civil-försvarsstyrelsen.)

Total by year and sex.

	1966/67	1976/77	1986/87
WOMEN	1	2	2
MEN	18	32	38
TOTAL	19	34	40
% OF TOTAL			
WOMEN	5.3%	5.9%	5.0%
MEN	94.7%	94.1%	95.0%

Source: Sveriges Statskalender 1967, page 241-242.
Sveriges Statskalender 1977, page 121-124.
Sveriges Statskalender 1986, page 129-130.

In 1966/67 the National Board of Civil Defence, Rescue
and Fire Services was subordinated to the Ministry of
Interior (inrikesdepartementet).

In table B3.7 the following are included:
The Board (incl. the Director-General (=the Chairperson),
two representatives of the staff (only 1976/77 and 1986/87)
(personalföreträdare)>, the Deputy Director-General (ställ-
företrädande chef>, Heads of Divisions (byråchefer), Heads of
Civil Defence Establishments (anläggningschefer), Head of
Policy Planning (planeringschef), Head of Production (prod.-
chef), Administrative Director (kanslichef) and Principal
Administrative Officers (aud.dir.).

(B3.8) NATIONAL BOARD OF PSYCHOLOGICAL DEFENCE.
(Styrelsen för psykologiskt försvar)

Total by year and sex.

	1966/67	1976/77	1986/87
WOMEN	1	2	0
MEN	14	15	9
TOTAL	15	17	9
% OF TOTAL			
WOMEN	6.7%	11.8%	0.0%
MEN	93.3%	88.2%	100.0%

Source: Sveriges Statskalender 1967, page 243-244.
Sveriges Statskalender 1977, page 124.
Sveriges Statskalender 1986, page 132.

In table B3.8 the following are
included: The Board (incl. the
Director-General (=Chairperson)) and Head
of Division (1966/67) (byråchef); Administrative
Director (1976/77) (kanslichef); Principal Adm.
Director (1986/87) (aud.dir.).
The women are members on the board.
In 1966/67 this authority was subordinated to
the Ministry of the Interior (inrikesdep.).

(B3.9) NATIONAL BOARD OF ECONOMIC DEFENCE.
(Överstyrelsen för ekonomiskt försvar)

Total by year and sex.

	1966/67	1976/77	1986/87
WOMEN	0	0	5
MEN	14	42	41
TOTAL	14	42	46
% OF TOTAL			
WOMEN	0.0%	0.0%	10.9%
MEN	100.0%	100.0%	89.1%

Source: Sveriges Statskalender 1967, page 232.
Sveriges Statskalender 1977, page 285.
Sveriges Statskalender 1986, page 131-132.

In table B3.9 the following are the Director
included: The Board (incl. the Director
General (=Chairperson) and two representatives of the staff (only 1976/77 and
1986/87) (personalföretr.)>,
Deputy Director-General, Heads of Divisions
(byråchefer), Principal Administrative
Officers (Aud.dir.).
In 1966/67 the authority was subordinated to
the Ministry of the Interior.

(B3.10) OFFICE OF THE DIRECTOR, REGIONAL CIVIL-IAN DEFENCE AREA. (Civilbefälhavare)

Total by year and sex.

	1966/67	1976/77	1986/87
WOMEN	0	0	0
MEN	12	12	17
TOTAL	12	12	17
% OF TOTAL			
WOMEN	0.0%	0.0%	0.0%
MEN	100.0%	100.0%	100.0%

Source: Sveriges Statskalender 1967, page 779.
Sveriges Statskalender 1977, page 989-990.
Sveriges Statskalender 1986, page 139-140.

In table B3.10 the following are
included: Directors, Regional Civilian
Defence Areas (six areas) (civilbefäl-
havare), Administrative Directors
(1976/77 and 1986/87) (kanslichefer)
and Principal Administrative Officers
(1966/67 and 1986/87) (aud.dir.).

(C) DECISION-MAKING BODIES DEALING WITH DISARMAMENT-ISSUES.

(C3) CENTRAL GOVERNMENT AUTHORITIES (Authorities subordinated to the Ministry for Foreign Affairs.)

(C3.1) THE DELEGATION OF DISARMAMENT (Nedrustningsdelegationen).

The Delegation of Disarmament started as a Ministerial Committee in May 1976. Today (1987) it is a permanent decision-making body at the Ministry for Foreign Affairs. The figures "Start" shows the number of members in May 1976. The figures "End" shows the number of members in December 1986. (See also explanation first in Appendix 28.)

The members of the decision-making body by position and total, by sex.

	Permanent members		Special Advisers		Experts		Secretariate		TOTAL	
	Start	End	Start	End	Start	End	Start	End	Start	End
WOMEN	2	3	-	-	2	3	0	0	4	6
MEN	9	7	-	-	10	17	1	1	20	25
TOTAL	11	10	-	-	12	20	1	1	24	31
% OF TOTAL										
WOMEN	18.2%	30.0%	-	-	16.7%	15.0%	0.0%	0.0%	16.7%	19.4%
MEN	81.8%	70.0%	-	-	83.3%	85.0%	100.0%	100.0%	83.3%	80.6%

Source: Start: Kommittéberättelsen 1977, page 57-42.
End: Kommittéberättelsen 1987, page 41-42.

The Chairperson was a woman both at "Start" in 1976 and at "End" in 1986. (Not the same person.)

(D) DECISION-MAKING BODIES DEALING WITH ISSUES CONCERNING FOREIGN AFFAIRS AND FOREIGN AID.

(D3) CENTRAL GOVERNMENT AUTHORITIES (Authorities subordinated to the Ministry for Foreign Affairs.)

(D3.1) THE SWEDISH INTERNATIONAL HUMANITARIAN LAW DELEGATION (Folkrättsdelegationen).

The Swedish International Humanitarian Law Delegation started as a Ministerial Committee in July 1972. Today (1987) it is a permanent decision-making body at the Ministry for Foreign Affairs. The figures at "Start" shows the number of members in July 1972. The figures at "End" shows the number of members in December 1986. (See also explanation first in Appendix 28.)

The members of the decision-making body by position and total, by sex.

	Permanent members		Special Advisers		Experts		Secretariate		TOTAL	
	Start	End	Start	End	Start	End	Start	End	Start	End
WOMEN	1	0	0	-	0	0	0	0	1	0
MEN	1	9	7	-	3	7	5	1	16	17
TOTAL	2	9	7	-	3	7	5	1	17	17
% OF TOTAL										
WOMEN	50.0%	0.0%	0.0%	-	0.0%	0.0%	0.0%	0.0%	5.9%	0.0%
MEN	50.0%	100.0%	100.0%	-	100.0%	100.0%	100.0%	100.0%	94.1%	100.0%

Source: Start: Kommittéberättelsen 1973, page 103-104.
End: Kommittéberättelsen 1987, page 40.

In 1972 only the Chairperson and Deputy Chairperson here included as Permanent Members. The Chairperson was a woman. The Experts and the Secretariate here appointed in August 1972. There were no Special Advisers in December 1986.

(D) DECISION-MAKING BODIES DEALING WITH ISSUES CONCERNING   (D3) CENTRAL GOVERNMENT AUTHORITIES (Authorities
    FOREIGN AFFAIRS AND FOREIGN AID.   subordinated to the Ministry for Foreign Affairs.)

(D3.2) THE SWEDISH INTERNATIONAL DEVELOPMENT AUTHORITY (SIDA)

(D3.2a) Total by year and sex.

	1966/67	1976/77	1986/87
WOMEN	2	8	17
MEN	26	41	46
TOTAL	28	49	63
% OF TOTAL			
WOMEN	7.1%	16.3%	27.0%
MEN	92.9%	83.7%	73.0%

Source: Sveriges Statskalender 1967. page 90-91. (Jan 67)
        Sveriges Statskalender 1977. page 86-88. (Jan 77)
        Sveriges Statskalender 1986. page 99-100. (Jan 86)

In the tables D3.2a and D3.2b the following are included:
The Board of the authority ("Board")
The Head Officials ("Heads")
Officials responsible for processing issues ("Proc.").

The following are included in the Board: Permanent members and the
Director-General (Generaldirektören) who is the Chairperson on the Board.
In 1976/77 and 1986/87 are two people who represent the officials
(personalföreträdare) also on the Board.

The following are included in Head Officials: The Deputy Director-
General (ouverdir. Generaldirektörens ställföretr.), Heads of Departments
(Avdelningschefer), Head of Divisions (Byråchefer), Chief Engineer (Överingenjör) Special Advisers (only 1976/77) (Sakkunniga, Teknisk rådgivare,
endast 1976/77) Head Information Officer (only 1966/67) (Informationschef,
endast 1966/67).

The following are included in the officials responsible for processing
issues (beredande, handläggande, personal): Principal Administrative
Officers (avdelningsdirektörer).

(D3.2b) Positions of members, by year and sex.

(D3.2ba) 1966/67.

	Board	Heads	Proc.	Total
WOMEN	1	1	0	2
MEN	8	11	7	26
TOTAL	9	12	7	28
% OF TOTAL				
WOMEN	11.1%	8.3%	0.0%	7.1%
MEN	88.9%	91.7%	100.0%	92.9%

Source: Sveriges Statskalender 1967, page 90-91.

(D3.2bb) 1976/77.

	Board	Heads	Proc.	Total
WOMEN	3	3	2	8
MEN	8	15	18	41
TOTAL	11	18	20	49
% OF TOTAL				
WOMEN	27.3%	16.7%	10.0%	16.3%
MEN	72.7%	83.3%	90.0%	83.7%

Source: Sveriges Statskalender 1977, page 86-88.

Two people who represent the officials are on the
Board, both were men. In the "Heads" three Advisers
are included, one woman and two men.

(D3.2bc) 1986/87.

	Board	Heads	Proc.	Total
WOMEN	3	5	9	17
MEN	11	13	22	46
TOTAL	14	18	31	63
% OF TOTAL				
WOMEN	21.4%	27.8%	29.0%	27.0%
MEN	78.6%	72.2%	71.0%	73.0%

Source: Sveriges Statskalender 1986, page 99-100.

Two people who represent the officials are on the
Board, one woman and one man.

(D) DECISION-MAKING BODIES DEALING WITH ISSUES CONCERNING FOREIGN AFFAIRS AND FOREIGN AID.

(D3) CENTRAL GOVERNMENT AUTHORITIES (Authorities subordinated to the Ministry for Foreign Affairs.)

(D3.3) SWEDISH BOARD FOR EDUCATION IN INTERNATIONAL DEVELOPMENT (Nämnden för U-landsutbildning).

Total by year and sex.

	1966/67	1976/77	1986/87
WOMEN	-	0	4
MEN	-	7	6
TOTAL	-	7	10
% OF TOTAL			
WOMEN	-	0.0%	40.0%
MEN	-	100.0%	60.0%

Source: Sveriges Statskalender 1977, page 88.
Sveriges Statskalender 1986, page 100.

This authority was established in 1971. Between 1971 and 1981 the Swedish name was "Biståndsutbildningsnämnden".

The Board and Administrative Director (one person) (kanslichef) are included in table D3.3.

(D3.4) CONSULTATIVE COMMITTEE ON HUMANITARIAN ASSISTANCE. (Beredningen för humanitärt bistånd)

Total by year and sex.

	1966/67	1976/77	1986/87
WOMEN	1	1	2
MEN	6	9	19
TOTAL	7	10	21
% OF TOTAL			
WOMEN	14.3%	10.0%	9.5%
MEN	85.7%	90.0%	90.5%

Source: Sveriges Statskalender 1967, page 92.
Sveriges Statskalender 1977, page 88.
Sveriges Statskalender 1986, page 101.

This authority was established in 1964. Until 1969 the Swedish name was "Beredningen för studiestöd till afrikansk flyktingungdom". In 1969 it changed name to "Beredningen för studiestöd och humanitärt bistånd till afrikanska flyktingar och nationella befrielserörelser". In 1978 it got it's present name "Beredningen för humanitärt bistånd". Both in 1969 and 1978 it's directives were somewhat changed.

Only the Board is included in table D3.4.

(D3.5) ADVISORY COUNCIL ON DEVELOPMENT-COOPERATION ISSUES (Beredningen för U-landsinformation).

Total by year and sex.

	1966/67	1976/77	1986/87
WOMEN	-	0	4
MEN	-	10	9
TOTAL	-	10	13
% OF TOTAL			
WOMEN	-	0.0%	30.8%
MEN	-	100.0%	69.2%

Source: Sveriges Statskalender 1977, page 88-89.
Sveriges Statskalender 1986, page 101.

The decision-making body has established in 1973.

Only the Board is included in table D3.5.

SUMMARY OF DECISION-MAKING BODIES - THE DIPLOMATIC SERVICE AND DELEGATIONS.

TABLE 1: The Diplomatic Service and Delegations. Number of and Per Cent Women, by Year. All Included Members*.

NAME OF DECISION-MAKING BODY	NUMBER OF WOMEN			PER CENT WOMEN			TOTAL NUMBER OF MEMBERS*			No of table
	1966/67	1976/77	1986/87	1966/67	1976/77	1986/87	1966/67	1976/77	1986/87	
Ambassadors	1	0	2	1.8%	0.0%	2.6%	55	63	76	(D3.6.1)
Permanent Mission of Sweden to the United Nations, New York	0	0	0	0.0%	0.0%	0.0%	7	8	8	(D3.7.1A)
Sweden's Permanent Mission to the Intern. Org. in Geneva	0	0	0	0.0%	0.0%	0.0%	4	4	4	(D3.7.1B)
Swedish Delegation to the Confe-rence on Disarmament, Geneva	-	0	0	-	0.0%	0.0%	-	2	1	(D3.7.1C)
ALL DECISION-MAKING BODIES	1	0	2	1.5%	0.0%	2.2%	66	77	89	
NOT INCL. AMBASSADORS	0	0	0	0.0%	0.0%	0.0%	11	14	13	

* Both men and women.

NOTICE: Notice that 4 delegations not are included in the above table. See tables D3.7.2, D3.7.3, D3.7.4 and D3.7.5 in Appendix 3B.

THE DIPLOMATIC SERVICE AND SWEDISH DELEGATIONS ABROAD
(Subordinated to the Ministry for Foreign Affairs.)

(D3.6) THE DIPLOMATIC SERVICE.

(D3.6.1) Ambassadors, by year and sex.
(Ambassadörer)

Total by year and sex.

	1966/67	1976/77	1986/87
WOMEN	1	0	2
MEN	55	63	76
TOTAL	56	63	78
% OF TOTAL			
WOMEN	1.8%	0.0%	2.6%
MEN	98.2%	100.0%	97.4%

Source: Sveriges Statskalender 1967, page 304-333.
Sveriges Statskalender 1977, page 429-467.
Sveriges Statskalender 1986, page 345-371.

In some cases one person is Ambassador in more than one country. In table D3.6.1 are these persons only counted one time.

(D3.7.1C) SWEDISH DELEGATION TO THE CONFERENCE ON DISARMAMENT IN GENEVA.
(Sveriges nedrustningsdelegation i Genève).

Total by year and sex.

	1966/67	1976/77	1986/87
WOMEN	-	0	0
MEN	-	2	1
TOTAL	-	2	1
% OF TOTAL			
WOMEN	-	0.0%	0.0%
MEN	-	100.0%	100.0%

Source: Sveriges Statskalender 1977, page 459.
Sveriges Statskalender 1986, page 571.

The Ambassador and the First Secretary (1976/77)/the Counsellor (1986/87) are included in table D3.7.1C. In 1986/87 the post as counsellor was unoccupied. The Swedish Delegation to the Conference on Disarmament belong to Sweden's Permanent Mission to the International Organizations in Geneva.

(D3.7) SWEDISH DELEGATIONS ABROAD

(D3.7.1) SWEDEN'S PERMANENT MISSIONS ABROAD (Sveriges permanenta delegationer i utlandet).

The permanent delegations of Sweden are nine. In the statistical data here compiled only two are included. For information about the remaining seven see the sources "Sveriges Statskalender (SS) 1967" page 315, "SS 1977" page 459-460 and "SS 1986" page 571-572.

(D3.7.1A) PERMANENT MISSION OF SWEDEN TO THE UNITED NATIONS, NEW YORK. (Sveriges ständiga representation vid FN, New York.)

Total by year and sex.

	1966/67	1976/77	1986/87
WOMEN	0	0	0
MEN	7	8	8
TOTAL	7	8	8
% OF TOTAL			
WOMEN	0.0%	0.0%	0.0%
MEN	100.0%	100.0%	100.0%

Source: Sveriges Statskalender 1967, page 314.
Sveriges Statskalender 1977, page 459.
Sveriges Statskalender 1986, page 571.

The Ambassador, Ministers (1986/87), the Counsellor, the Military Adviser, the Pressattaché (1986/87 and 1966/67) and First Secretaries (1976/77 and 1966/67) are included in the table D3.6.1.

(D3.7.1B) SWEDEN'S PERMANENT MISSION TO THE INTERNATIONAL ORGANIZATIONS IN GENEVA.
(Sveriges ständiga delegation vid de internationella organisationerna i Genève.)

Total by year and sex.

	1966/67	1976/77	1986/87
WOMEN	0	0	0
MEN	6	4	4
TOTAL	6	4	4
% OF TOTAL			
WOMEN	0.0%	0.0%	0.0%
MEN	100.0%	100.0%	100.0%

Source: Sveriges Statskalender 1967, page 315.
Sveriges Statskalender 1977, page 459.
Sveriges Statskalender 1986, page 571.

The Swedish Delegation to the Conference on Disarmament in Geneva is not included in table D.7.1B, although it formally belong to Sweden's Permanent Mission in Geneva. See table D3.7.1C. The Ambassador, the Counsellors, the Minister (1986/87), the Press-Attaché (1966/67 and 1976/77) and the First Secretaries (1966/67 and 1976/77) are included in table D3.7.1B.

THE DIPLOMATIC SERVICE AND SWEDISH DELEGATIONS ABROAD
(Subordinated to the Ministry for Foreign Affairs.)

(D3.7.2) SWEDISH DELEGATIONS TO THE EUROPEAN CONFERENCE
OF SECURITY AND COOPERATION 1973 - 1987.

Total by year and sex.

	Helsinki	Belgrad	Madrid	Stockholm	Vienna
WOMEN	0	1	0	4	1
MEN	5	7	9	15	3
TOTAL	5	8	9	19	4
% OF TOTAL					
WOMEN	0.0%	12.5%	0.0%	21.1%	25.0%
MEN	100.0%	87.5%	100.0%	78.9%	75.0%

Source: The Ministry for Foreign Affairs, Stockholm, Sweden.

Notes:
Helsinki: The figures show permanent members (ombud) of the
delegation to the follow-up negotiations in Geneve, September
1973 and July 1975. The delegation also included ten advisers
of which one was a woman (10%).
Belgrad: The figuress show permanent members to the main
meeting in Belgrad 1977. To the preparatory meeting there
were two delegates, one man and one woman (50%).
Madrid: The figures shows the delegates to the main meeting,
first session November-December 1980. To the second, third and
fourth session, January-December 1981, there were 10 delegates,
of which one was a woman (10%). To the fifth and sixth session,
February-March 1982 and November 1982-September 1983, there were
three and four delegates, respectively, all men.
Stockholm: The figures show the permanent members who where delegates
from the beginning. Two persons, both men, became permant members of
the delegations during the period of the conference: January 17,
1984 - September 19, 1986. The delegations also had four experts from
the beginning, of which one was a woman (25%). Four other persons,
all men, joined the delegations as experts during the period.
Vienna: The figures show permanent members of the delegation to the
follow-up meeting in Vienna 1986-1987.

(D3.7.4) TWO SPECIAL SESSIONS OF THE UNITED NATIONS GENERAL
ASSEMBLY OF DISARMAMENT, 1978 AND 1982.

Total by year and sex.

	1978	1982
WOMEN	3	3
MEN	8	6
TOTAL	11	9
% OF TOTAL		
WOMEN	27.3%	33.3%
MEN	72.7%	66.7%

Notes:
1978: Period May 23 - July 1, 1978.
      18 adviser, one woman (6%).
1979: Period June 7 - July 10, 1982.
      13 advisers, no women.

Source: The Ministry for Foreign Affairs, Stockholm, Sweden.

(D3.7.5) THE SWEDISH DELEGATION TO THE WOLRD CONFERENCE
OF DISARMAMENT AND DEVELOPMENT, UNITED NATIONS,
NEW YORK, Augusti 1987, by sex.

	1987
WOMEN	3
MEN	5
TOTAL	8
% OF TOTAL	
WOMEN	37.5%
MEN	62.5%

Notes:
Eight advisers, one woman (12%).

Source: The Ministry for Foreign Affairs, Stockholm, Sweden.

(D3.7.3) SWEDISH DELEGATIONS TO THE UNITED NATIONS
GENERAL ASSEMBLY, FIRST COMMITEE 1978 - 1986.

Total by year and sex.

	1978/79	1979/80	1980/81	1981	1982	1983	1984	1985	1986
WOMEN	7	5	4	6	3	7	6	7	6
MEN	12	12	13	14	17	13	14	13	13
TOTAL	19	17	17	20	20	20	20	20	19
% OF TOTAL									
WOMEN	36.8%	29.4%	23.5%	30.0%	15.0%	35.0%	30.0%	35.0%	31.6%
MEN	63.2%	70.6%	76.5%	70.0%	85.0%	65.0%	70.0%	65.0%	68.4%

Source: The Ministry for Foreign Affairs, Stockholm, Sweden.

Notes: All figures show permanent members (ombud) and substitutes for the permanent
members (ersättare for ombud).
1978/79: Period Sept. 19 - Dec. 21, 1978 and January 15-29, 1979. The delegation also
included 30 advisers, of which one was a woman (3%).
1979/80: Period Sept. 18, 1979 - January 7, 1980. 31 advisers, of which two women (6%).
1980/81: Period Sept. 16, 1980 - January 16, 1981. 31 advisers, of which one woman (3%).
1981: Period Sept. 15 - Dec. 18, 1981. 28 advisers, of which two women (7%).
1982: Period Sept. 21 - Dec. 21, 1982. 31 advisers, of which two women (6%).
1983: Period Sept. 20 - Dec. 20, 1983. 36 advisers, of which one woman (3%).
1984: Period Sept. 18 - Dec. 18, 1984. 33 advisers, of which three women (9%).
1985: Period Sept. 17 - Dec. 18, 1985. 33 advisers, of which four women (12%).
1986: Period Sept. 16 - Dec. 19, 1986. 38 advisers, of which seven women (18%).